PROSECUTING
NAZI WAR CRIMINALS

PROSECUTING NAZI WAR CRIMINALS

Alan S. Rosenbaum

Westview Press
BOULDER • SAN FRANCISCO • OXFORD

Copyright © 1993 by Westview Press, Inc.

Published in 1993 in the United States of America by Westview Press, Inc., 5500 Central Avenue, Boulder, Colorado 80301-2877, and in the United Kingdom by Westview Press, 36 Lonsdale Road, Summertown, Oxford OX2 7EW

Library of Congress Cataloging-in-Publication Data
Rosenbaum, Alan S.
   Prosecuting Nazi war criminals / Alan S. Rosenbaum.
      p.   cm.
   Includes index.
   ISBN 0-8133-8357-9 (hc) — ISBN 0-8133-3287-7 (pb)
   1. War crime trials.   2. World War, 1939–1945—Atrocities.
I. Title.
JX5436.R67   1993
940.53'18—dc20   92-46912
                                                                                      CIP

Printed and bound in the United States of America

 The paper used in this publication meets the requirements of the American National Standard for Permanence of Paper for Printed Library Materials Z39.48-1984.

10   9   8   7   6   5   4

To those who continue the fight against
antisemitism, racism, religious bigotry,
and all other forms of persecution
wherever and whenever they occur

CONTENTS

PREFACE

During the 1930s, in what started as an official policy of discrimination and repression against German Jewish citizens, and building on a long tradition of antisemitism,[1] the Nazi government of the German Third Reich created a cultural and legal environment in which Jewish-owned property throughout Germany was defaced, burned, or stolen, and random violence and persecutions against Jews became widespread. In 1941, this official process of vengeance for the "Jewishness" of being Jews took a historically unique turn: the deliberate and systematic devastation of Jewish culture and of European Jewry, i.e., the "Final Solution" to the so-called Jewish Problem. This series of events has become known as the Holocaust (in Hebrew, *Shoah*). Its culmination: Over 11 million people were put to death by the Third Reich government and its collaborators and sympathizers, not because of something they did or did not do, but because of who they were. Six million Jewish people were systematically liquidated; and for this reason alone, the Holocaust has been seen as a Jewish-centered event, though many millions of gentiles also died.

Almost fifty years later, a practical challenge now confronts us as a legacy of the Nazi Holocaust: How are we to deal with those remaining individuals who are believed to have committed atrocities but who have evaded the prosecution process? Many Nazi party members and collaborators fled the Third Reich (though many remained) as it collapsed in 1945, settling in other parts of Europe, in South America, in the Middle East, in Canada or in Britain, and in the United States, and they assumed new lives and new identities and assimilated into the cultural mainstream of their host countries. It is also true that many former Nazis who are still alive have managed to evade any form of legal accountability and have maneuvered themselves into legitimate positions of authority and social responsibility, e.g., in medicine, law, politics, business, and education.

Many questions arise—in law, public policy, and philosophy—regarding the value and wisdom of prosecuting or seeking to prosecute these individuals. Moreover, the tasks of locating and apprehending fugitive Nazi criminals, gathering sufficient evidence to prosecute them, and eventually placing them on trial are all extremely cumbersome, expensive, and contentious, especially when the harboring nations are uncooperative. Although such noncooperation has been a continuing issue since the end of World War II and the Nuremberg trials, official attention is now focused on certain countries whose governments are reluctant or have refused to bring to trial or to extradite for trial any such suspects in their midst (e.g., Alois Brunner in Damascus under the protection of the Syrian government). The trials of John Demjanjuk (in the United States and then in Israel) and Klaus Barbie (in France) in the 1980s continue to inflame issues, and controversies surround the question of prosecution, which have been addressed dramatically in the press, in official political circles, in court, and in the classroom. In these circumstances, some have contended that the Nazi criminals should be allowed to die in peace and relative obscurity, whereas other sources insist that suspects be brought to face an official system of justice designed to address the legal ramifications of their actions. Even among those who advocate prosecution, disputes exist about who should prosecute whom on what grounds and ultimately whether continued prosecutions are a good thing.

After World War II, it should be noted, the prosecution of prominent Nazis at Nuremberg raised important moral and philosophical questions about the trial's "legal" basis. These questions were raised because the victorious Allies believed that the establishment of legal precedents would avoid the appearance of a vengeful retribution—instead of legal justice—by the victors on the vanquished. Because no international *criminal* court of justice was in existence at the war's end, or has been established since then, it was virtually unavoidable that the following questions would confront prosecutors: Under whose and what law(s) would the suspects be tried? On what authority can law-abiding citizens of one state be held accountable for behavior deemed illegal and/or flagrantly immoral by other states? And were the Allies in violation of their own constitutional principles by trying the Nazis under ex post facto rules? "War crimes," "crimes against humanity," "crimes against peace," and international law were invoked. Ultimately, the prosecution argued that the Hitlerian decrees, the Nuremberg laws, and the Nazi judicial system were "criminal" from an international point of view; hence, their enactment and enforcement were nothing more than complicity in crime.[2]

Similar kinds of questions about the legal basis of war crimes prosecutions followed in the wake of the Coalition victory over Iraq in 1991. Such questions will continue to plague those who believe the Iraqi soldiers and leadership under Saddam Hussein ordered and committed atrocities against the Kuwaiti people during its short-lived invasion and occupation of Kuwait and should therefore be brought to justice.

Although none of the responses to these inquiries during and after Nuremberg has settled matters once and for all time, or to every reasonable person's satisfaction, they all have become part of the historical record and so have assumed weighty standing in the official tradition.

In this book I will examine the foregoing questions and other related issues. I will argue that the prosecution process *itself* is a moral, legal, and political necessity.

The prosecution process is a series of events through which a suspected criminal is identified, and evidence is gathered of sufficient extent to warrant either an official indictment by a grand jury or by some other charging instrument. In criminal judicial proceedings, it is a basic postulate that insufficient evidence terminates the prosecution process in the sense meant here; however, investigatory activities may continue for some crimes. Although the question of punishment resulting from conviction in such cases bears directly on the nature of the crime and on the sort of nonrepressive ideal society we envision for ourselves, it will be addressed, as I believe it should be, only as an issue separate from prosecution. The philosophical and juristic concept of the rule of law will also be analyzed because it is shown to be essential to the cardinal thesis of my book: that *not* bringing suspected Nazi criminals to trial is flagrantly immoral and a serious assault on the basic values of civilization and on the conception of a democratic, rights-based society.

NOTES

1. I use the spelling "antisemitism," not the conventional "anti-Semitism," to refer to the anti-Jewish nature of certain attitudes, actions, and policies. Since Arabs are also a Semitic people, the conventional usage seems inappropriate.

2. Louis Henkin et al., eds., *International Law: Cases and Materials* (St. Paul: West, 1980), pp. 248–52. For the present task, I will sidestep a study of the question of whether certain isolated acts done by the Americans in the conduct of the war were also "war crimes." See, e.g., Clay Blair, Jr., *Silent Victory* (New York: Lippincott, 1975), pp. 354–55.

Alan S. Rosenbaum

ACKNOWLEDGMENTS

I wish to thank the many people listed below who assisted me in any number of ways with the preparation of my book. Any errors that the book contains are solely mine.

Spencer Carr, editor, Westview Press; John Russell, research director, Department of Justice, Office of Special Investigations; John Roth, professor of philosophy, Claremont McKenna College; Benjamin Ferencz, Nuremberg prosecutor; Whitney Harris, Nuremberg prosecutor; Henry King, Nuremberg prosecutor; Aaron Breitbart, research director, Wiesenthal Documentation Center, Los Angeles, California; Efraim Zuroff, director, Wiesenthal Documentation Center, Jerusalem, Israel; Judge Leo Glasser, Federal District Court, Eastern New York; Judge Frank J. Battisti, U.S. District Court, Northern District of Ohio; Dr. Suzannah Heschel, Distinguished Professor, Case Western Reserve University; Rabbi Arthur Lelyveld; Professor Herbert Hockhauser, director, Ohio Council of Holocaust Education at Kent State University; Clifford Savren, director, Anti-Defamation League, Cleveland, Ohio, Division; and librarians Dr. Ralph Simon, Temple EmanuEl, Cleveland, Ohio, and Marie Rehmar, Reference Services, Cleveland-Marshall College of Law. And I owe a special debt of gratitude to Cindy Bellinger, our department secretary.

A.S.R.

1

INTRODUCTION

In this book I propose to defend the thesis that the continuation of earnest efforts at prosecuting fugitive Nazi war criminals is an urgent moral imperative. The main reason for the assertion of a moral necessity behind my thesis is the indefeasible connection existing between the discharge of such an obligation and respect for basic moral values and principles of justice, social order, and democracy. A failure to fulfill this obligation by permitting the Nazi offenders to evade justice will be shown to violate the values and principles that bring an ideal standard and meaning to our lives as morally autonomous social beings. There is a supervening affirmative duty to prosecute the doers of serious offenses that falls on those who are empowered to do so on behalf of a civilized community. This duty corresponds to our fundamental rights as citizens and as persons to receive and give respect to each other in view of our possession of such rights. Dealing seriously with rights (and values and principles), i.e., fulfilling duties to others, entails dealing seriously with rights violations. As I will explore throughout this book, it is clearly a flouting of such a basic obligation to fail to bring Nazi persecutors to justice, especially by allowing rebuttable considerations like time and resource expenditures, and the dying off of remaining Nazi war criminals (and their surviving victims), to influence whether or not they get prosecuted.

Indeed, the urgency for pressing the case for prosecution, though secondary to the main argument, I believe springs from two sources. First, the population of surviving fugitives from justice is diminishing rapidly, and soon all the perpetrators as well as their surviving victims will perish by natural attrition. After all, it has been almost a half century since the commission of the Nazi crimes. Second, the unique evil of the Holocaust compels the political and judicial authorities in our generation to confront in a high-minded manner the question that future generations will ask about the rectitude of our generation's response: Did we do what was necessary to bring to justice those who committed the Nazi atrocities?

As the immediate poignancy of the Holocaust recedes into historical perspective, the growth of the postwar generations overwhelms the few remaining survivors in the totality of the world's population. The immense volume of indisputable documentation about what happened in the Holocaust is accessible, coherent, and reliable. The problem, then, is not what occurred but rather how the enormities of the Third Reich are to be *remembered*. I take this concern to be of paramount importance in framing my arguments for sustained prosecutions of Nazi war criminals. For in holding the perpetrators of the most serious of crimes accountable for their actions, we also demonstrate the seriousness with which we respect such considerations as the principles of justice.

Arguments that oppose the continuation of the process of prosecution, some of which stem from Holocaust deniers or have been resurrected from those marshaled against the original wave of trials at Nuremberg (1945–1946), have an attractive veneer of reasonableness, particularly to the increasingly large numbers of younger people who have little or no knowledge of the genuine nature and dimensions of the Holocaust. Therefore, my assessment of the various arguments relating to bringing Nazi criminals to justice must be framed within a context that characterizes or highlights the most egregious facets of the Holocaust.

In the next chapter, I offer a brief overview of the Holocaust. Philosophically it is important to suggest, at least in part, that the special nature of the Nazi crimes, coupled with the official accountability of the offenders, should constitute a paradigm case of the universal significance of prosecuting Nazi criminals for prosecuting future offenders suspected of serious wrongdoing. In Chapter 3, I explore certain aspects of the aftermath of the defeat of Hitler's Third Reich, including the Nuremberg trials and related legal and political issues such as the charge of "victor's justice" and the overall fairness of the concept and proceedings. In Chapter 4, I characterize a rights-based, democratic concept of the rule of law and contrast it with some core features of the Nazis' legal system. The concept of the rule of law will be used to further support my argument in favor of continuing to prosecute all remaining Nazi war criminals. Chapter 5 deals with the Nazi fugitives and their postwar escape from accountability. The general contours of their escape will suggest not only the complexity involved in tracking these people down but also the legal, political, and moral difficulties in bringing them to trial. In Chapter 6, I explore the questions about responsibility: Who is responsible for prosecuting Nazi war criminals, and who was responsible (either morally and/or legally) for the Holocaust and, in the end, who is to blame, morally and legally. Finally, I address a set of recurrent arguments against prosecuting Nazi war criminals and mount a rebuttal to these claims.

In general, if my book contributes to the clarification of (what I believe is) the compelling moral case that these prosecutions ought to continue, it will have served its primary purpose. And perhaps, through promoting more successful prosecutions, it will reveal how the moral bond between past and future generations may be strengthened. It will indicate that for all those who perished in the Holocaust, "we in the present generation have not forgotten you." But also, to those who were responsible for the Nazi persecutions, "you, too, have not been forgotten!" In this vein, I am reminded of a "war" poem that may be interpreted as a metaphorical call to discharge the special obligation I believe we have in the wake of the Holocaust to restore a certain moral equilibrium:

Take up our quarrel with the foe:
To you from failing hands we show
The torch; be yours to hold it high.
If ye break faith with us who die
We shall not sleep though poppies grow
in Flanders fields.[1]

As we reflect in more general philosophical terms about our connection today to these events of the 1930s and 1940s, what do we tell ourselves and allow to be told about the Holocaust? And when our children and our children's children inquire about the Holocaust, an important recurring question is what will our generation teach them about how the Nazi genocidists and their collaborators were dealt with? Did we forgive them ex parte in the absence of any official regret or even acknowledgment by them of wrongdoing? Did we ignore or allow the persecutors who survived and escaped official accountability to assume positions of standing in respectable society? Were they permitted or even helped to resettle in some safe haven or to establish false identities, if necessary, to ensure their not being detected? Did we conscientiously bring to trial all those for whom justiciable evidence could be gathered? Successful prosecutions of Nazi war criminals not only do justice and provide a document of who did what to whom but, in addition, bolster our commitment to upholding—for us and the younger generations— our most cherished values by bringing to account those who assaulted them by advancing and implementing an anti-Western ideology based (among other things) on war and genocide.

In this vein, it is increasingly common for uninformed younger people born after the defeat of the German Third Reich to ask: What did the Nazis do that was so terrible that may explain or justify—so many years later—the pursuit of remaining Nazi fugitives to bring them to justice? Historical revisionism trades on such ignorance. Since the Holocaust occurred while the Nazi Reich was at war, it mistakenly appears or is made to appear to some people to have been a natural part of the war effort. For in the immortal words of General William Sherman, "War is hell!" Accordingly, whatever combatants do to one another in the course of hostilities can only be explained and even excused as *essential* to war. Yet, this reasoning goes, things sometimes do get out of control, and excesses are committed; but this is what war is, "war is hell."

Although I deal with the established rules of war in Chapter 3, a terse reply to this hidden but specious assumption (that war explains if not excuses all acts done in its name or under its cover) that lies behind the aforementioned—and perhaps innocent—question is the following. In the first wave of prosecutions against the Nazi leadership at Nuremberg, the charges against the defendants clearly distinguished between the essentials of war, i.e., the range of suitable conduct in furtherance of the aims of war and, on the other hand, crimes against humanity, crimes of aggression and war crimes. These crimes were regarded as a significant violation of established rules of war (see Chapter 4) and universal standards of morality. So in response to the question about what the Nazis did to warrant such charges and efforts to prosecute Nazi fugitives, the standard reply is that they masterminded and implemented a strategy to exterminate systematically the Jews of occupied Europe, viz., the Holocaust, and they also persecuted and murdered many millions more, including Gypsies, Slavs, Poles, the handicapped, gays, and political dissidents.

DEFINITIONS

Before I give an overview of the Holocaust, the term itself requires definition. The term has evolved from its earlier religious connotations of a "sacrifice wholly consumed by fire" (*The Oxford English Dictionary*, 1989) of a global conflagration to "the earth being burnt to a cinder in nuclear war" and finally to its current usage, the Nazis' so-called Final Solution to the Jewish Question: or the deliberate systemative "destruction of European Jewry."[2] However, the term has been used—or misused—to characterize diverse instances of suffering, e.g., the legacy of black slavery in the United States, the internecine slaughter of Cambodians under the Pol Pot regime, the Turkish genocide against the Armenians, and, ironically, the plight of Palestinians in relation to Israel; and some religious zealots have used it in reference to abortion. In short, the term has been applied to almost any instance of widespread suffering. These various applications of the term are not without dispute. Nor am I inclined to argue that these instances of suffering are somehow less worthy of consideration than the suffering of the Jewish people in the Holocaust. Without impugning the motives of those who deliberately inflate the meaning of the term "Holocaust" (unless it is clear that Jewish suffering is being downgraded for antisemitic reasons), I believe that it is intended as a paradigm of *human* suffering. This is not to suggest that Jewish suffering has "moral primacy" over the sufferings of other individuals or peoples, as if to diminish the horrors non-Jews have experienced. Rather, in the interest of fairness and truth, it is necessary to catalogue both the similarities and differences among cases of catastrophic suffering, thereby giving each case its due. Therefore, I would prefer to underscore the usage that has been reserved for the Nazi genocide against the Jews while stressing the universalizing character of the enormity of certain crimes like the Holocaust that human beings under quite specific circumstances and conditions can visit upon their fellow beings.

One other tack I shall note seeks to merge the Holocaust into the stream of universal abstractions such as "man's cruelty to man" or "human suffering." In doing so, the term tends to lose its special character, and even becomes trivialized. In fact, there is what seems to be a natural tendency among some of my colleagues in professional philosophy to find or bestow value on things only insofar as they can be categorized, subsumed, or construed as mere instances of a more general thing of importance. For example, causal historical explanations of the Holocaust that are encased in generalized abstractions like "human actions" (in R. G. Collingwood's idealist theory) or "insanity" (associated with positivism's hierarchy of laws) or even Hitler's weltanschauung end up explaining very little of consequence or nothing.[3] As such, the enduring value of the Holocaust is calibrated by its conceptual proximity or similarity to other similar expressions of the generalized abstraction. In this way, nothing "unique" or "singular" or paradigmatic remains of the Holocaust. In my view, giving full recognition to the unique evil of the Holocaust—in both event and name—one people's suffering ought to be seen as an essential condition for acknowledging the equally immoral suffering other people are made to endure.[4]

In the overview in Chapter 2, the universal implication of the Holocaust, as I intend it, is that it is a clear illustration of how people can do atrocious things to other people if preventive measures and conditions are not in place. In this sense, the Holocaust may be "a generic name for an ideologically motivated planned total murder of a whole people," but it is to date the worst case of genocide in this century. Yet an argument may be made that the Armenian genocide by the Turks (1914–1918) is sufficiently similar to the Holocaust so that the latter cannot be singled out as unique. The problem with this claim, despite a number of obvious parallels, is that it ignores the important differences between the two cases, viz., that the Turks, on the one hand, not only murdered Armenians within Turkey for practical reasons of political power but did so in violation of their own moral standards. The Nazis, on the other hand, killed Jews by moral imperative through a process of summary execution or ingathering from all occupied territories and then murdering them, the motive being that the Jews were regarded as *the* obstacle to world progress. The Turks never intended to wipe out the seed of the Armenian people everywhere, whereas the Nazis intended by murder to make the world "Jewish-free." In summary, the Armenian genocide ought to be placed on the "continuum of evil" closest to the Holocaust because of the motivation to murder an entire people.[5]

Two other terms require definition before I proceed: "genocide" and "Nazi war criminal." The term "genocide" was coined by a Polish Jew, Raphael Lemkin, to give a label to the kind of murders associated with the Holocaust and to distinguish it from other types of murder (e.g., individual murders, serial murders, mass murders, and so forth). Lemkin was influential in conceptualizing "genocide" for the United Nations' *Convention on the Prevention and Punishment of the Crime of Genocide.*[6] By "genocide" he meant "the destruction of a nation or of an ethnic group . . . it does not necessarily mean the immediate destruction of a nation. . . . It is intended rather to signify a coordinated plan of different actions aiming at the destruction of the essential foundations of the life of national groups, with the aim of annihilating the groups themselves."[7]

As understood by Lemkin, the crime of genocide centers on the aim or intention of the genocidist. But there are grounds for questioning the adequacy of his definition. For instance, D. Lackey has claimed that genocide is sufficiently like any common murder of a person or any political mass murder such as the Syrians did to the population of the city of Hamas or the Iraqis did to the civilians of Kuwait (my examples). Intentions in these instances are qualitatively similar, Lackey presumably argues. Thus as the perpetrators' intentions are morally indistinguishable, so from the victim's viewpoint, "my loss is the same either way."[8] Given Lackey's moral individualism, systematic murder, which was the goal of the Holocaust, is significantly similar to the use of murder as a means toward an end to achieve its purpose such as the Colombian drug cartel murders of government officials to weaken the government's war on drug traffic. Finally, Lackey observes that "in terms of terror, the thought that I am being killed because someone believes that I stand in the way of some further good is just as overwhelming as the thought that I am being killed because someone believes the world would be better off without me."[9]

R. Brecher has challenged Lackey's view of genocide in relation to the Holocaust on the ground that it fails to distinguish the qualitatively different intentions of the Nazis, viz., the intention to kill all members of a class of people from the intentions at play in other types of murder. In support of Brecher's argument, we may refer to the "battered wife" defense in the case of a murdered husband in contrast to the deliberate killing of innocent civilians in an act of terrorism (such as the downing of an airliner over Lockerbee, Scotland). And so, Brecher may claim, contra Lackey, that there are important moral differences—and not only in terms of the moral character of an act—and that the Nazi genocide is, like terrorism, morally worse because of the nature of its consequences.[10] Brecher holds that the peculiar moral quality of genocide resides in its consequences:

> It is something which no human being can take steps to avoid by modifying their beliefs, attitudes or behavior; it is something which might happen to anyone; and . . . it . . . happens to them because of what they happen to be. Is this not a greater threat to humanity than even the mass murder of people on account of what they think, believe or do just because . . . there is no avoiding it?[11]

In "locating the Holocaust on the genocide spectrum," it "is measured not by the events of 1933 [viz., the original intent of the Nazi regime—my parenthetical comment] but by the results achieved in 1945. The product of twelve years of anti-Semitism was the nonexistence of European Jewry."

I agree with H. Huttenbach when he observes that "to list this crime alongside crimes that were not genocidal . . . would be a disservice to the goal of clarification."[12] He offers a broader definition of genocide: "any act that puts the very existence of a group in jeopardy."[13] The advantage of Huttenbach's definition over others that focus on the agent's character or intentions, or on the consequences of genocidal actions (because they distinguish between types of genocide and not merely acts of genocide or nongenocidal acts of murder) is that there is no mention of the perpetrator, of the kinds of groups, of the means used, nor of the genocidal evidence (except that accusations must be based on substantive evidence of genocide). In our quest to refine our meaning of genocide, it is hoped that we are enabled to get a more exact fix on the concept of the Holocaust. In any case, the concept of genocide was initially introduced in the Nuremberg Tribunal indictment (October 18, 1945) that charged the Nazi defendants with the "crime of deliberate and systematic genocide."[14] The crime of genocide was defined in a resolution (260, A, III) passed by the General Assembly of the United Nations, which stated: "genocide is the denial of the right of existence to entire human groups."

According to a later convention of the United Nations, genocide "is committed with the intent of destroying wholly or partly a national, ethnical, racial or religious group as such."[15] It is not merely an "intent" that will qualify an action as a crime of genocide for it must also include the "will to annihilate," coupled with the deliberate execution of a planned scheme.

Accordingly, S. Friedlander quotes the words of a German historian, E. Jäckel:

> The National Socialist murder of the Jews was unequalled because never before has a State, with the authority of its responsible leaders, decided and announced the total killing of a certain group of people, including the old, the women, the children, the infants, and turned this decision into fact, with the use of all the possible instruments of power available to the state.[16]

This, then, is a summary of the unparalleled genocide that the "Holocaust" is meant to signify.

A third, important term or phrase that requires definition is "Nazi war criminal." It has been well defined by E. Zuroff (Director, Israel Office, Simon Wiesenthal Documentation Center) "as a person who assisted in the persecution of innocent civilians during World War II, in the service of or in collaboration with the forces of Nazi Germany."[17] Zuroff indicates that the number of such criminals is minimally in the hundreds of thousands. His estimate includes "the German-Austrian machinery of annihilation and countless collaborators in every country occupied by the Third Reich as well as in the satellite states."[18] Zuroff's definition enjoys a certain advantage because its restrictive focus undermines the concept of collective guilt in favor of a case-by-case, (individual) justiciable accountability. Indeed, this was the official U.S. position at the Nuremberg trials. It was articulated by Justice Robert H. Jackson when he said that "we have no purpose to incriminate the whole German people. We know that the Nazi party was not put into power by a majority of the German vote."[19]

Retrospectively, however, I think that responsibility for participation at some discernible level in the pattern of persecutions, "atrocities, massacres, executions," and expropriations of property suggests that, in reality, the scope was too narrowly drawn at Nuremberg. This theme concerning the problem of blame will be examined at some length in Chapter 6. In general, it is important to recognize that the Nuremberg trials were designed to handle cases involving only some of the Nazi bigwigs; some of the others were to be prosecuted in domestic courts. Nonetheless, we should note that these relatively few individuals could not have carried through the murderous policies of the Nazi regime without assistance and cooperation from all levels of the "nazified" populations.

NOTES

1. J. McCrae, "In Flanders Fields," in J. Silkin, ed., *First World War Poetry* (Baltimore: Penguin Books, 1979), p. 85.

2. David Roskies, *Against the Apocalypse* (Cambridge: Harvard University Press, 1984), pp. 261, 346n.

3. See Emil Fackenheim, "Holocaust and *Weltanschauung:* Philosophical Reflections on Why They Did It," *Holocaust and Genocide Studies*, vol. 3, no. 2 (1988), pp. 197–208.

4. Peter J. Haas, in *Morality After Auschwitz*, (Philadelphia: Fortress Press, 1988), seeks to grasp the Holocaust in a way that avoids what he considers are the pitfalls of "uniqueness" and "banality." But in his effort to salvage the lessons of the Holocaust, the only enduring links he finds, as I read him, are those atrocities that can be seen as "universal." I believe Haas misses or dismisses the unique character of the Holocaust.

5. Yehuda Bauer, *A History of the Holocaust* (New York: Franklin Watts, 1982), p. 332; Yehuda Bauer, "The Place of the Holocaust in Contemporary History," in John K. Roth and Michael Berenbaum, eds., *Holocaust: Religious and Philosophical Implications* (New York: Paragon House, 1989), pp. 31–35.

6. The United States became the ninety-seventh signatory when it ratified the Convention in 1988. See Louis Henkin, *The Age of Rights* (New York: Columbia University Press, 1990), pp. 21, 75.

7. Raphael Lemkin, *Axis Rule in Occupied Europe* (Washington, D.C.: Carnegie Endowment of International Peace, 1944), p. 79.

8. Douglas Lackey, "Extraordinary Evil or Common Malevolence?: Evaluating the Jewish Holocaust," *Journal of Applied Philosophy*, vol. 3, no. 2 (1986), p. 171.

9. Ibid.

10. Robert Brecher, "Learning from the Holocaust," in Yehuda Bauer et al., eds., *Remembering for the Future,* vol. 2 (Oxford: Pergamon Press, 1989), pp. 1830–31.

11. Ibid., p. 1835.

12. Henry Huttenbach, "Locating the Holocaust on the Genocide Spectrum," in Bauer et al., *Remembering for the Future*, vol. 2, p. 2034.

13. Ibid., p. 2033.

14. Quoted in Yves Ternon, "The Will to Annihilate for an Approach to the Concept of Genocide," in Bauer et al., *Remembering for the Future*, vol. 2, p. 2060.

15. Ibid.

16. Saul Friedlander, "On the Representation of the *Shoah* in Present-day Western Culture," in Bauer et al., *Remembering for the Future*, vol. 3, p. 3095.

17. Efraim Zuroff, "Recent Efforts to Prosecute Nazi War Criminals Living in Western Democracies—Successes and Failures," in Bauer et al., *Remembering for the Future*, vol. 3, p. 2806.

18. Ibid. Also see Bruce F. Pauley, *From Prejudice to Persecution: A History of Austrian Antisemitism* (Chapel Hill: University of North Carolina Press, 1992), pp. 275–333.

19. *Trial of the Major War Criminals Before the International Military Tribunal,* Nuremberg, November 14, 1945–October 10, 1946; vol. 2, pp. 102–3.

2

THE HOLOCAUST: AN OVERVIEW

The Nuremberg trials were a cardinal source of information about the Holocaust. They revealed a broad pattern of complicity the dimensions of which

> shook the complacency of a Western culture that had overestimated the depth of its civilized qualities. The Holocaust was the story of the planned mass murder of populations of children; old people; men and women; of Jews, Gypsies, and Slavs; of prisoners of war; of soldiers and civilians killed not in the heat of combat but in convoys or actions over a period of years as a policy, a duty to the race. Witnesses and detailed documents at the trials told of a return to slavery and organized plunder on an enormous scale; of institutions such as hospitals and courts of law designed to assuage human pain and injustices that had been warped to the purpose of inflicting them. A total of 80,000 technicians of slaughter had been involved in the extermination process, it was calculated, but to make their operations possible in the wide reaches of the empire of the Great German Reich, a well-trained bureaucracy and a superb army had been required too, as well as the cooperation, willing and unwilling, of millions of people in Germany and the occupied territories.[1]

The core of the Holocaust was the single-minded effort by the Nazi organization to round up all of the Jews of Europe and to deport ("resettle") them to the forced labor and/or death camps. A review of some of the fateful occurrences that eventuated in the Nazi "Final Solution to the Jewish Question" will demonstrate that the exterminative activities were the outcome of, among other factors, a virulent antisemitism.

A few months after the Nazi accession to power and the appointment of Hitler as Reich chancellor in 1933, the Nazi Sturmabteilungen (SA; Storm Troopers) organized a nationwide boycott of Jewish-owned businesses.[2] The effect of this action was violence against both person and property, but it also resulted in dismissal from jobs of many Jews throughout Germany, including professionals (professors, journalists, lawyers, and government personnel). The Nazi-influenced police forces deliberately and consistently refrained from protecting those Jews under attack.

In 1935, some "legal" measures were introduced in the Reich that were directed against Jewish religious practice, inheritance, and citizenship. The infamous Nuremberg laws were enacted legalizing discrimination against all German Jews, i.e., they lost all their civil rights. The Reich Citizenship Law made race a key consideration in the determination of citizenship. The impact was to deny to Jews any participation in the official life of Germany.[3] Also, the Law for the Protection of German Blood and Honor (the so-called Purity of German Blood law) prohibited marriage and sexual relations between Jews and "pure-blooded, Aryan" Germans. According to these laws, even the German flag, that symbol of nationality, could no longer be flown above Jewish homes.[4]

The Nazis had used the legal system to isolate and repress the Jews and to steal their property. The aryanization of the German economy, like the "voluntary" emigration, had not succeeded in ridding Germany of its Jewish people. Further, the impact of Polish antisemitism had made itself felt in the highest echelons of the Nazi leadership when the Polish government refused to repatriate the Polish Jews in Germany who sought to return. These stateless Jews were seen as a burden on the Reich.

An internal power struggle among the competing Nazi forces was a factor in the widespread violence that traumatized the German Jewish community in 1938 when, using the expediency of the assassination of a secretary in the German embassy in Paris by a Jewish youth (who was enraged that his parents were so mistreated by the German authorities), the Jews *as a people* were blamed for the murder. Their penalty has come to be called *Kristallnacht* (the night of the shattered glass). Hundreds of synagogues were set ablaze, in some instances with congregants still inside the buildings.

Glittering shards of glass from windows were strewn about the streets throughout Germany as businesses still associated with Jews were ransacked and burned. Many thousands of Jews were arrested and sent to concentration camps. Many were beaten, women were raped, and some people were killed. This "pogrom," or random mob violence, against Jews was the final such impulsive event in the streets of Germany.[5]

Neither bureaucratic pressure nor terror were successful in convincing Jews in large enough numbers to emigrate from Germany and Austria (which was annexed by Germany in 1938), as I have already noted. Representatives of thirty-two nations held a meeting, the Evian-les-Bains Conference, a few months before *Kristallnacht,* which accomplished very little in trying to solve the plight of the Jews in the greater German Reich. Most participants would not revise upward their immigration quotas to permit more Jewish people to leave. Instead, they tried to persuade

Germany to alleviate the conditions of Jews from within the Reich. In effect, the failure of Evian to assist the Jews, coupled with Germany's desire to rid itself of Jews, conspired to impress the Nazi government that nobody really cared about the Jews. Indeed, they were considered a "surplus people."[6]

The officially sponsored mass murder of the Jews, the Holocaust—which has come to be symbolized by its largest death camp—Auschwitz, became virtually inevitable owing to the cover of war and, among other things, the external indifference, vicious antisemitism, and the empowerment of "the instrument of the Final Solution": the *Schutzstafeln* (defense squad; SS).

Under SS administration, many of the concentration camps were transformed into killing centers. As Pearl Harbor was being bombed by the Japanese, the Germans had begun to murder the Jewish internees at Chelmno, the first murder facility in operation. Mobile vans were utilized to gas the victims. Thus Nazi persecution had resulted in the beginning of the fulfillment of "a world without Jews."

In early 1942, another fateful conference was held at Wannsee where preparations were being made by the Nazis to systematically exterminate the declared enemy of the German *volk* (people)—the Jewish people. Whole communities of Jews from distant places throughout Europe such as Greece, Croatia, and Romania were deported to the death camps but not without the Nazis and their accomplices stealing all artwork and personal belongings of any value, from shoes and clothing to rings, hair, and even the gold pried from the teeth of corpses. Some Jewish deportees were coerced into unpaid labor and when injured or exhausted, sent to their deaths.

Mass murder by means of gas or injection was already in use in the Third Reich to rid Germany and Austria of thousands of children whose physical deformities or mental incapacities made them ill suited for a place among a "racially healthy" *volk*. Medicalized murder of "racially unhealthy" adults—the so-called mercy deaths of the insane and deformed and the terminally ill—had taken the lives of tens of thousands of people.[7] What distinguished the Nazi "mercy deaths" from the conventional idea of euthanasia, or even physician-assisted suicide, is that the latter cases are usually the result of the patient's informed consent, after all possibilities of remediation have been exhausted and with the patient unable to endure pain. However, the Nazi murder mission of mercy was for the state's advantage and not the patient's.[8]

Generally, the emergence of racial politics and medicine was no accident. For example, the Nuremberg race laws were primarily associated with a physician (Gerhard Wagner). In the words of one contemporary physician, "the SS physician on the railroad ramp at Birkenau was a consequence of a paradigm having its roots in legitimate and acceptable medical policies and practices" in the German Reich. Physicians saw themselves as, and cast themselves in the role of, selector, experimenter and exterminator. It is the doctor "who decides on the differential value of human life."[9] SS physicians on duty at Auschwitz, as the railroad cars unloaded the Jewish "patients," made selections on the basis of what they determined to be "useful life" or "useless life." The prescription for the former was enslavement as a laborer in Auschwitz's industrial complex; for the latter, the gas chamber and crematoria. Behind this portrait was the physician's role in Nazi Germany. The doctor was a medical agent whose primary responsibility is to the state and not to the patient. Moreover, racial pedigree as a Jew became a metaphor in Nazi Germany for virulent disease; only quarantine in ghettos and then extermination could ultimately cleanse and heal society.[10]

This medical exercise of antisemitic racialism was reinforced by a more historically and culturally pervasive hatred against the Jews inspired by the myth that the Jews, both individually and collectively, are to be held perpetually (and in the first instance) responsible for the death of Jesus (i.e., "murderers of the Lord"). S. Wiesenthal writes:

> The segregation of the Jews, their ghettoization, stigmatization, and indescribable humiliation (as it was practiced by the National Socialists from the very beginning) can be traced back to the Christians, primarily to militant Catholics. The popes—the representatives of Christ on earth—have admittedly never called for the destruction of the Jews, but they welcomed their degradation, because in the humiliated Jews the world could see proof of the punishment that is visited upon all those who reject Jesus.[11]

Indeed, scandalous characterizations of the Jewish people as inferior, subhuman, and parasitic have enjoyed a long history in Europe.[12] The crucial conceptual add-on of dangerousness was needed to complete the picture of a people who were to be regarded as less than human. In my opinion, subhumans are useful merely for work, whereas deadly parasites destroy their host and so must be either controlled or eliminated in the interest of health. It may be said that such ideas were not directly responsible for motivating people to murder other people. Rather, they helped to create a poisoned climate of ill will and insensitivity to the fate of such beings.

Although the intended annihilation of the Jews was a Hitlerian first principle as early as his writing of *Mein Kampf* in 1925, the history of anti-Jewish persecution that eventually helped to sire the deed of mass murder was less than continuous, as one observer notes.[13] Yet when the ideological-religious instigation of hatred combined with the assumption of dictatorial power, bureaucratic administration, modern technology, and the cover of war and with the accessibility of a Jewish minority as a scapegoat for socioeconomic ills,[14] they constituted the indispensable elements that forged the Holocaust.[15] It was Hitler's power to act and not merely to speak that gave new meaning to the words he spoke in early 1939: "Today I want to be a prophet once more: if international-finance Jewry inside and outside of Europe should succeed once more in plunging nations into another world war, the consequence will not be the Bolshevization of the earth and thereby the victory of Jewry but the annihilation *Vernichtung* of the Jewish race in Europe."[16] However, even Hitler had to be assured that there was no other alternative but the "Final Solution" (note his efforts to compel mass emigration before 1920–1921). In 1941 in a letter Hermann Göring wrote to R. Heydrich, the "Final Solution" was at hand. And with this letter, exchanged between high-ranking Nazi officials, observes R. Hilberg, the "centuries-old policy of expulsion was terminated and a new policy of annihilation was inaugurated."[17] Hilberg concedes, though, that the mention of a "final solution" did not explicitly denote murder for in the letter the term remained undefined. But it soon became clear in conversations with Heydrich that the Jews were to be liquidated.[18]

To engineer the Holocaust, the bureaucratic administration involved

> identity cards; registration lists and files; skillful propaganda aimed at lulling the Jews into a false sense of security; specialist killing squads coordinated by the apparatus of the state; concentration camps and ghettoes; armed anti-Semitic brigades enrolling local policemen and civilian volunteers; death camp gas chambers and crematoria; serial numbers tattooed on camp inmates; sadistic medical experiments and concerted measures to dehumanize Jews; a continent-wide bureaucracy to track down and kill every Jewish survivor; and the expertise of every professional group in Germany, including diplomats and lawyers, engineers and physical scientists, medical doctors and biologists, economists and anthropologists, and soldiers and railroaders.[19]

And, I would add, the directors of some of the largest business corporations.

The benefits of dictatorship for carrying ideology and policy into effect are patently ingredient in the monopoly of power and control. Bureaucracy refers generally to the network of functionaries who execute the commands of the Nazi institutional authorities. Bureaucracies tend to exact compliance while relieving their agents of personal responsibility for the impact of their actions or decisions; after all, they were "merely following orders." Before the Holocaust, the technical impossibility of mass murder on the scale of genocide usually reduced Jewish degradation to three alternatives: convert, be expelled, or die. The Nazi technology was sufficiently developed to murder those people in the millions whom the Nazis declared were "unfit to live."[20] The Holocaust resulted in the deaths of almost two-thirds of the European Jews and one-third of the Jews of the world.[21] For never before had a government organized its nation into a hate and scientific murder machine directed against the Jewish people.[22]

As we reflect on this uniquely evil event, the Holocaust, our collective memory fades along with the vividness of the firsthand accounts given to us by a passing generation of eyewitnesses to and victims of the Nazi terror. What gives chilling effect to this thought is the report of a conversation Simon Wiesenthal, the famed pursuer of fugitive Nazi criminals, had with an SS leader during the Nuremberg trials. The SS leader recalled a discussion that had taken place between Adolf Eichmann and a group of SS in 1944. One SS member asked Eichmann how many Jews had been killed. "About 5 million." Then another SS leader, who had no illusions anymore about the coming end of the war and its outcome, asked: "What will happen when the world asks about these millions of dead?" Eichmann apparently snapped back: "One hundred dead are a catastrophe, one million dead are nothing but a statistic."[23]

Under the cover of war, the Nazis sought to keep secret the mass murders, "with the hope that final victory would 'justify' the crimes."[24] The paths of persecution that led to Auschwitz are numerous, and they merged into what has become a moral watershed in history. The Jewish-centered nature of the Holocaust, despite the millions of other victims—Gypsies, Russian POWs, gays, political enemies, enslaved workers—has moral implications for humanity. It also may be adjudged a paradigm of human suffering. Nevertheless, as one scholar notes, no other victims "were singled out for total destruction or pursued so relentlessly throughout occupied Europe as were the Jews."[25]

NOTES

1. Eugene Davidson, *The Trial of the Germans* (New York: Collier Books, 1966), pp. 7–8.

2. Raul Hilberg, *The Destruction of the European Jews* (New York: Harper Torchbooks, 1961), p. 62.

3. Raul Hilberg, ed., *Documents of Destruction* (Chicago: Quadrangle Books, 1971), pp. 18–25.

4. Richard L. Rubenstein and John K. Roth, *Approaches to Auschwitz* (Atlanta: John Knox Press, 1987), p. 113.

5. Hilberg, *The Destruction of the European Jews*, pp. 20–29; also Robert E. Conot, *Justice at Nuremberg* (New York: Harper and Row, 1983), pp. 163–75.

6. Rubenstein and Roth, *Approaches to Auschwitz*, pp. 123–25.

7. Robert Jay Lifton, *The Nazi Doctors* (New York: Basic Books, 1986), pp. 14–102.

8. Rubenstein and Roth, *Approaches to Auschwitz*, p. 143.

9. William Seidelman, "Medical Selection," in Yehuda Bauer et al., *Remembering for the Future*, vol. 2 (Oxford: Pergamon Press, 1989), p. 1308.

10. Of course, Adolph Hitler's own book, *Mein Kampf*, trans. Ralph Manheim (Boston: Houghton Mifflin, 1943), has contributed mightily to this notion. See, e.g., pp. 305, 327.

11. Simon Wiesenthal, *Every Day Is Remembrance Day* (New York: Henry Holt, 1987), p. 15.

12. For a historical and thematic analysis of some of the important contributors to the antisemitic Germanic ideology, see Fritz Stern, *The Politics of Cultural Despair* (New York: Anchor Books, 1965), passim; also, Peter Viereck, *Meta-Politics: The Roots of the Nazi Mind* (New York: Capricorn Books, 1961), passim; Richard M. Lerner, *Final Solutions: Biology, Prejudice and Genocide* (University Park, Pennsylvania State University Press, 1992); Paul L. Rose, *Revolutionary Antisemitism in Germany: From Kant to Wagner* (Princeton: Princeton University Press, 1990); and Robert S. Wistrich, *Antisemitism: The Longest Hatred* (New York: Pantheon Books, 1991).

13. John Roth, "How to Make Hitler's Ideas Clear," *Philosophical Forum*, vol. 16, no. 1-2 (Fall-Winter 1984–1985), p. 93.

14. Yves Chevalier, "The Holocaust as a Paroxystic Form of a Scapegoat Strategy," in Bauer et al., *Remembering for the Future*, vol. 2, p. 1350.

15. Wiesenthal, *Every Day Is Remembrance Day*, pp. 11–28.

16. Raul Hilberg, *The Destruction of the European Jews*, p. 257.

17. Ibid., p. 262. See also Richard Breitman, *The Architect of Genocide* (New York: Knopf, 1991), for a study of Heinrich Himmler's major contribution to genocide.

18. Ibid., p. 263, n. 32.

19. Frank Chalk, "Definitions of Genocide and Their Implication for Prediction and Prevention," in Bauer et al., *Remembering for the Future*, vol. 3, pp. 2377–78.

20. Wiesenthal, *Every Day Is Remembrance Day*, p. 20.

21. Rubenstein and Roth, *Approaches to Auschwitz*, p. 158.

22. *Trial of Major War Criminals Before the Nuremberg Military Tribunal*, vol. 1 (Nuremberg, 1947), pp. 33, 870–71.

23. Wiesenthal, *Every Day Is Remembrance Day*, p. 29.

24. Ibid., p. 22.

25. Lee Gibbs, "The Historicity of the Holocaust and the Historical Jesus," *Gamut*, no. 31 (Winter 1991), pp. 4, 16, n. 1.

3

THE AFTERMATH
OF THE THIRD REICH

THE NUREMBERG TRIALS:
BRINGING WAR CRIMINALS TO JUSTICE

In the aftermath of World War II, with the defeat of the two main Axis powers (Germany and Japan), the governments of the victorious Allied nations agreed to establish special "international" courts at Nuremberg and Tokyo for the purpose of placing on trial some of the major Nazi and Japanese war criminals. The historical uniqueness of the Nuremberg trials was prompted by the response of the Allies to the grotesque nature of the crimes committed. It was a blend of universal moral standards with an evolving body of international law inspired by the moral outrage felt by the international community, despite some initial disagreements about how to treat such criminals.[1] In any case, it was intended that legal responsibility be fixed for the atrocities that were committed under or by the Nazi and Japanese military and political leadership. Among the reasons the Nuremberg location was selected was its notoriety for the earlier Nuremberg laws for the "racial purification of the greater Reich."

Actually there were four different criminal proceedings associated with the expression "Nuremberg trials." Twenty-four high-ranking Nazis were indicted and brought to Nuremberg to stand trial before the International Military Tribunal (IMT).

The IMT was authorized by the London Charter (part of an agreement reached by the Allies in 1945 specifying the powers and duties of the IMT) and was presided over by judges from the United States, the Soviet Union, Great Britain, and France. This first trial took place between October 18, 1945, and October 1, 1946. Only twenty-two defendants were tried eventually because one was too ill to stand trial and the other committed suicide. Only some of the surviving leaders of Nazi Germany were to be found in the dock at the first Nuremberg trial. Each was selected because he was the most important surviving principal in his domain of responsibilities and activities for the Third Reich. Included in this group were such infamous luminaries as Reichs-marshall Hermann

Göring, German air force commander and Hitler's designated successor; Rudolph Hess, Hitler's deputy; Ernst Kaltenbrunner, the Gestapo chief; Julius Streicher, editor of *Der Stürmer*, a purveyor of endless antisemitic propaganda; and Hans Frank, governor-general of occupied Poland. All were hanged except Hess, who died in prison, and Göring, who committed suicide the night before his planned execution. (It has been argued persuasively at a reunion of the Nuremberg prosecution team in March 1991 in Washington, D.C., that the cyanide tablet Göring used was evidently smuggled to him by an impressionable U.S. soldier who had access to his cell.) Although the IMT was called a "military tribunal," the court's intention was to sit in lawful judgment of the people who were guilty of planning, carrying out, and organizing, or commanding others to commit, war crimes. The reason that the term "international" was incorporated in the IMT designation was to underscore "the universal validity of its judgment and its importance for the entire world."[2] Nevertheless, a stigma of vengeful retribution by the victor over the vanquished has persisted to this day and so has impugned to some minimal extent the legitimacy of the trials. However, the IMT originally addressed this matter, which I will discuss in due course.

A second set of trials also took place at Nuremberg, the so-called Subsequent Nuremberg Proceedings authorized by Control Council Law No. 10 (December 20, 1945), in which 177 SS, Sicherheitsdienst (SD), Gestapo, SA,[3] industrialists, civil servants, physicians, and members of other groups or organizations alleged to have been of a criminal character were placed on trial. At the request of the prosecutors, the IMT found that some organizations were criminal by their very nature, thereby facilitating prosecution of individuals belonging to such organizations.[4] Tokyo was the site for the third type of Nuremberg trial. The East Asian IMT was composed of a multinational panel of eleven judges. The fourth Nuremberg trial consisted of a series of judicial proceedings held either in proximity to the scenes of the crimes, in liberated areas, or in former Axis territory controlled by the victorious Allies.[5]

In retrospect, we can fully appreciate the task faced by Associate Justice of the United States Supreme Court, Robert H. Jackson, as he accepted President Harry Truman's assignment to become the U.S. chief of counsel in the forthcoming war crimes trials. It was his job in bringing the criminal Nazi leadership to justice to

> obtain the agreement of the allies to a military trial; negotiate with them the organization, jurisdiction, and procedure of the tribunal; join with them in the identification of the persons to be accused and to prepare suitable indictments; find a site for the trial, see to the availability of a courtroom, prison and other facilities for the trial; supervise the housing and feeding of

lawyers and others participating in the trial; and find the members of his legal staff and personally conduct and direct the prosecution of the case on behalf of the United States.[6]

And this he did, in a short span of eighteen months, by all accounts masterfully seeing the trial through to its conclusion. To distinguish his view from the contrary British position, viz., to summarily execute the Nazi leadership, Justice Jackson stated his preference for the primacy of the rule of law: "The ultimate principle is that you must put no man on trial under the form of judicial proceedings, if you are not willing to see him freed if not proved guilty. If you are determined to execute a man in any case, there is no occasion for a trial. The world yields no respect to courts that are merely organized to convict."[7] Jackson's view ultimately prevailed, even against the Russian view that held that a war crimes trial should only evaluate the punishment to be meted out to those in the Nazi leadership whose criminal actions had already been determined; the purpose of the trial was not to determine guilt or innocence. The trial, of course, went forward with deliberate speed, fairness, and respect for the principles of international law.

The first wave of Nuremberg trials resulted in a guilty verdict for nineteen defendants, with a variety of sentences ranging from prison terms to death, and in three acquittals. These decisions indicate that the IMT did not merely impose penalties based on preconceived ideas of guilt, as the detractor's charge of "victor's justice" implies. It may be added that whatever procedural shortcomings may have plagued the Nuremberg proceedings, "rudimentary sanctions by a victor state are probably better than a situation where war criminals feel themselves exempt from any future prosecution."[8] (I will argue in Chapter 7 that this cogent utilitarian claim must nonetheless yield to a more important retributive argument, particularly from our perspective of a half-century later, for continuing the process of seizing and prosecuting fugitive Nazi war criminals.) In any case, the Allies were taught a very important lesson about "victor's justice" in the post—World War I period. After the Allies agreed to give the defeated Germans jurisdiction to prosecute their own war criminals, which they did in trials at Leipzig (1922), their dashed expectations that the Germans could be entrusted to try their own nationals with justice according to the rule of law demonstrated the folly of such recourse. It was reported that, at the urging of the Allies, the Germans indicted 901 of their leaders. Of these, 888 were either acquitted or had charges against them summarily dismissed because they or witnesses either could not be located or could not be compelled to appear in court. Those who were convicted received nominal sentences, and some among them were even permitted to escape from prison.[9] In view of the Leipzig debacle, it was likely that the war criminals of the future would be prosecuted by the victors or by the international community.

The complexity involved in planning the Nuremberg trials, despite their expeditious execution, suggests the importance that was attached by the Allies to making the proceedings more than an impromptu show trial. In fact, the intent to prosecute these war criminals at the proper time is expressed in a number of important, and early, official declarations by Allied governments. They include: the St. James Palace Declaration (January 13, 1942); the Moscow Declaration by the Three Powers (November 1943; the United States, England, and the Soviet Union paved the way at this conference for the eventual San Francisco conference in spring 1945, which set up the United Nations organization); the decision to establish the United Nations War Crimes Commission (London, 1943); and most importantly, the London Agreement (August 8, 1945), because it promulgated the landmark Charter of the International Military Tribunal. The London Charter condemned "war crimes," "crimes against humanity," and "crimes against the peace."[10]

A summary of the principles of international law acknowledged in both the Charter and the Judgment of the Nuremberg Tribunal was articulated by the International Law Commission (1950) of the United Nations:

Principle I: "Any person who commits an act which constitutes a crime under international law is responsible therefore and liable to punishment";

Principle II: The fact that international law does not impose a penalty for an act which constitutes a crime under international law does not relieve the person who committed the act from responsibility under international law";

Principle III: "The fact that a person who committed an act which constitutes a crime under international law acted as Head of State or responsible government official does not relieve him from responsibility under international law";

Principle IV: The fact that a person acted pursuant to order of his government or of a superior does not relieve him from responsibility under international law, provided a moral choice was in fact possible for him";

Principle V: "Any person charged with a crime under international law has the right to a fair trial on the fact and law";

Principle VI: "The crimes hereinafter set out are punishable as crimes under international law:

a. Crimes against peace:

(i) Planning, preparation, initiation or waging of a war of aggression or a war in violation of international treaties, agreements or assurances;

(ii) Participation in a common plan or conspiracy for the accomplishment of any of the acts mentioned under (i).

b. War crimes: Violations of the laws or customs of war which include, but are not limited to, murder, ill treatment, or deportation to slave labor or for any other purpose of civilian population of or in occupied territory, murder or ill treatment of prisoners of war or persons on the seas, killing of hostages, plunder of public or private property, wanton destruction of cities, towns, or villages, or devastation not justified by military necessity.

c. Crimes against humanity: Murder, extermination, enslavement, deportation and other inhumane acts done against any civilian population, or persecutions on political, racial or religious grounds, when such acts are done or such persecutions are carried on in execution of or in connexion with any crime against peace or any war crime";

Principle VII: "Complicity in the commission of a crime against peace, a war crime, or a crime against humanity as set forth in *Principle VI* is a crime under international law."[11] Crimes against humanity are regarded as actionable provided that they were perpetrated in relation to other crimes within the jurisdiction of the IMT; they do not stand on their own.

These Nuremberg principles are now considered international law by the United Nations (General Assembly Resolution 95 [I]) and represent the chief legacy of the trials. However, an additional charge made by the UN General Assembly to the International Law Commission was to explore the possibility of establishing a Criminal Chamber of the International Court of Justice (the Genocide Convention, 1949, Article XIX[B]). As of 1992, no such court has been organized, although the UN has established an international commission authorizing the investigation of the commission of such crimes in the former Yugoslavia. And for this reason, the prospects of a war crimes trial for Saddam Hussein of Iraq after his defeat in early 1991 are not very realistic, since the least unfeasible alternative confronting the victorious Allies is to convince the Security Council of the United Nations to draft a resolution creating an international criminal court. The other alternatives are even more improbable, each with its own weaknesses (e.g., a Kuwaiti war crimes trial will undoubtedly be seen as "victor's justice"; an agreement by the Coalition would be unlikely and virtually unworkable; agreement among Gulf Cooperation Council members is improbable because the council is too loosely organized, but also their sponsorship of such a trial would exclude the Western powers).[12]

Legal Justice, Not Vengeance

The charter of the IMT, though not completely identical in all specifics to the London Agreement, was the basis for the charges in the indictments against the individual defendants at Nuremberg. Not all defendants were charged on all possible counts, viz., (1) Common Plan or Conspiracy; (2) Crimes Against the Peace; (3) War Crimes; (4) Crimes Against Humanity.[13]

To show that it was not mere vengeful rage by the public that spontaneously erupted at the war's end that gave a veneer of legality to the trials, ostensibly because it was the victorious allies who set the terms for prosecuting Nazi war criminals, it is helpful to cite the lengthy evolution of informed opinion about the value of valid trials. Official governmental declarations by the United States and Great Britain surely played a large role in publicizing the Nazi atrocities as they were occurring. But other early indications of atrocities appeared in the print media, which helped to inform public opinion about the desirability of war crimes trials, not only to punish the guilty but also to get out the facts as evidence of guilt and to provide a historical record of exactly what happened. However, it was typical of the U.S. press to bury the stories relating to the Holocaust (at that time, a crime for which there was no name, said Winston Churchill) in the back pages. In one of the more uncharacteristically forthright reports, for instance, in one of New York's leading newspapers, the *New York Herald Tribune* (December 5, 1941), an article described the plight of European Jewry in Nazi-controlled territory as being "worse than a status of serfdom—it is nothing less than systematic extermination."[14]

The Holocaust as Portrayed in the Public Media

Much-deserved criticism has been leveled in the 1980s against the clear pattern of muted or restrained reportage during the war as the word of increasing and systematic atrocities by the Nazis and their accomplices leaked out. The *Nation* and the *New Republic* were among the few in the U.S. media to call for "a little less pity and a little more help" for European Jews.[15] We shall probably never know how many Americans realized a Holocaust was under way; but as one authoritative scholar indicates, despite the failure of the mass media to place the information unequivocally before the public eye, daily readers were able to discern a pattern of reported German atrocities against the Jews. For example, a Gallup poll in early 1943 showed that 47 percent of Americans believed the reports.[16] In bold contrast to the mainstream U.S. media, the full significance of "extermination" was made abundantly evident to the British public by the British press as early as 1943. "Here were the first public reports of gassing and the first reference to a systematic continent-wide program of murder," observes a prominent researcher.[17] A boldface headline in the *Daily Telegraph and Morning Post* read "Germans murder 700,000 Jews in Poland: Travelling Gas Chambers"; in the *London Times*, a headline read "Massacre of Jews—Over 1,000,000 Dead Since The War Began," and so on.[18] "Two weeks before the end of 1942, the Allied governments themselves confirmed the existence of a program for the annihilation of European Jewry."[19]

Instead of calling for some form of immediate action to halt the atrocities, some print media (in the United States) like the *New York World Telegram* would support . . . the creation of an Allied commission to identify the guilty so that *after* the war they could be punished" (December 11, 1942, p. 26).[20] Another isolated and early example is the *Atlanta Constitution* (December 18, 1942, p. 2), which did issue a call for trials to be held eventually, "not later than the end of the war."

There is no question that the gradual and mounting but well-founded revelations of systematic Nazi atrocities sensitized the U.S. public and others to the need for deserved justice, not simply retaliatory vengeance, against the perpetrators. Even as the cold-blooded murder of captured U.S. POWs by the Nazi SS Panzer regiment at Malmedy, Belgium, in December 1944 became known and outraged the public, the intensity of reactions eventually was translated into widespread support and an impetus for the prospect of war crimes trials. Although the public had clamored for punishment of the Nazi war criminals, most U.S. politicians understood that this meant the United Nations must be prodded for quick action. Since the UN War Crimes Commission was not charged with organizing summary executions but with collecting and collating documentation on war crimes and war criminals, the results of its investigations would be used by the prosecutors in the Nuremberg Trials.

President Franklin D. Roosevelt was fully informed about the Nazi extermination of the Jews by late 1942; but as Nobel Laureate Elie Wiesel stresses in his preface to D. Wyman's well-researched book, he "did nothing about the mass murder for fourteen months, then moved only because he was confronted with political pressures he could not avoid and because his administration was on the brink of a nasty scandal over its rescue policies."[21]

Finally, at the war's end, with almost 6 million Jews as well as many millions of others murdered by the Nazi regime, the trials were held. This was the first, and the last, time that war crimes trials were held by an *international* tribunal. Prosecutions of a comparatively small number of Nazi fugitives from justice have occurred since Nuremberg but only within the domestic jurisdiction of a few, individual nations. By 1950, the public's interest in further trials of war criminals had pretty well dissipated. By then, "about half of the top leadership of the SS . . . survived or disappeared. . . . Fewer than 1 million of the nearly 3.5 million persons charged before denazification courts were brought to trial, and of these only 9,600 . . . spent any time in confinement. By 1949 all but 300 had been freed."[22]

In order to explore some key legal and moral issues confronting the policymakers, judges, and lawyers at Nuremberg, we must first illumine some relevant historical background to the issues raised.

International Law and the Laws of War

One of the main sources of modern international law is found in the evolving body of rules for waging war. Cicero, the Roman statesman, once wrote that the "laws are silent amidst the clash of arms" (*Pro Milone*).[23] War (or the "clash of arms") has been defined in modern terms as "a sustained struggle by armed force of a certain intensity between groups, of a certain size, consisting of individuals who are armed, who wear distinctive insignia and who are subjected to military discipline under responsible command."[24]

If we accept this definition of war, it would seem that Cicero's observation is not very useful, though it does have some intuitive appeal. That is, during the course of hostilities, war makes civilization impossible. So in this sense, it seems that war is an inhuman or uncivilized series of acts, a breakdown of civilization. To the extent that law in its noblest conception is generally a product, protector, and promoter of civilization, the expression "laws of war" seems both counterintuitive and contradictory. Yet the manner in which the conduct of war is ideally constrained by international law today suggests that even war may be lawful, just, and to some degree, civilized.

In my view, war is sometimes a necessity, e.g., to thwart or remove an aggressor's warmaking power. In such cases, war is also just because there is a clear right to use armed force to repel or prevent serious threats to life and property. Hugo Grotius (1583–1645), a Dutch jurist who is often called the father of modern international law, had distinguished between just and unjust wars, the latter being unacceptable. Also writing in the natural law tradition, the eighteenth-century Swiss diplomat E. de Vattel developed Grotius's doctrine by claiming that only defensive wars are just whereas aggressive wars are unjust (again, a distinction absent in Cicero).[25] Contrary to Cicero, the notion that war has for centuries been governed ideally by certain "civilizing" rules and standards of conduct has a history rooted in custom and (and also common law) the so-called laws of nature, in which Cicero, too, believed; he merely interpreted them differently. In general, a realism seasoned by historical perspective dictates that the scourge of war is unlikely to be eradicated in the foreseeable future. Therefore, civilized people must seek to impose standards that nevertheless uphold the higher moral interests of humanity by regulating the manner and means by which war is fought.

In this way, even conduct during war can and ought to be judged on moral grounds.

Gratian, a twelfth-century medieval Italian monk who compiled canon law, stated that "the soldier who kills a man in obedience to authority is not guilty of murder." Accordingly, it is well recognized in principle, law, and practice that war confers a "blanket of immunity" over soldiers who commit acts that are criminal if done in peacetime ("killing, wounding, kidnapping, destroying or carrying off other peoples' property").[26]

However, some evidence seems to indicate that humane influence on how war is conducted has ancient roots. Some ancient societies, like Egypt and India, banned certain warfare methods and treatment of prisoners of war. Some medieval philosophers such as Augustine and Aquinas, along with some church leaders (Innocent III, Alexander III), influenced as the ancients did the evolution of the humane conduct of war. The rules of chivalry (enforced by English courts) were said to regulate war between knights. For instance, a story is told that when King "Richard the Lionheart's horse was killed, Sultan Saladin is said to have provided him with another one before they resumed fighting."[27] Humanizing influence on war also issued from secular sources like Casimir of Poland who legislated certain protections for war victims.[28]

If from ancient times it was a practice for the losers in armed combat to be treated barbarically, it may be claimed that some philosophers as well as some treaties among states have indirectly, if not directly, influenced thinking about and restraints on some of the crueler aspects of war. For example, Montesquieu did not repudiate a right of war but did argue that "conquest is an acquisition, and carries with it the spirit of preservation and use, not of destruction." He defines the right of conquest as "a necessary, lawful, but unhappy power, which leaves the conqueror under a heavy obligation of repairing the injuries done to humanity." Further, he writes: "It is a plain case that when the conquest is completed, the conqueror has no longer a right to kill, because he has no longer the plea of natural defence and self-preservation."[29] Montesquieu had thus envisioned in the eighteenth century an ideal limit on the scope of warmaking at the outset of any postwar period. An early nineteenth-century (and often-quoted) theoretician, C. von Clausewitz, claimed "that war is the continuation of politics by other means and is to be tempered by the demands of the very politics that have given rise to it in the first place."[30] In other words, he proposed that the legitimacy of armed conflict between nations hinged on proportioning hostilities to the purpose of war. He said: "The political object will thus determine both the military objective to be reached and the amount of effort it requires." Hence Clausewitz was an early articulator of the rightful limits to be imposed in the course of war.

Theoretically, the effect of this thinking about inherent limits on warfare is the notion that once conquered, the enemy must *not* be subjected to "unnecessary or revengeful destruction of life. . . . Plundering and devastation [are] . . . condemned as barbarous and uncivilized."[31] Some treaties and unilateral regulations concerning the treatment of noncombatants and prisoners of war reinforced the tendency toward laws governing warfare.

Humanitarian ideals also inspired some countries in the nineteenth century to issue codes about the conduct of war, e.g., that "unnecessary or revengeful destruction of life is not lawful" (Article 68, the so-called Lieber Code for Armies in the Field, 1863).[32] The Declaration of Paris (1856) by Europe's principal powers was a multilateral or international agreement on maritime war; it outlawed privateering (a practice whereby a government commissions a privately owned and armed vessel to make war against an enemy).[33]

Another significant development in maritime law—and more importantly for the present purpose, in the emergence of international criminal law—concerned the attempt by some nations to deal legally with the plague of piracy on the high seas. As feudalism became displaced by the mercantile system of Europe, protection of the free flow of commerce against acts of piracy acquired priority. Hence piracy was outlawed as the enemy of all humankind and of civilization, and pirates could be placed on trial wherever they might be seized.[34] This principle of "universal jurisdiction" affirms that certain crimes are universally condemnable and so obligate any or all members of the community of nations to seize and punish such criminals in the interest of all nations. Specific rules for the orderly regulation of international commerce were gradually developed, narrowing the scope of what could and could not be done legally in relations between nations and to nations.

Other contributing influences on the development of international law with respect to the laws of war and especially their impact on the Nuremberg war crimes trials came from certain declarations, conventions, and treaties. The St. Petersburg Declaration (1868) was a treaty signed by the main governments of Europe. They agreed to fix "the technical limits at which the necessities of war ought to yield to the requirements of humanity," i.e., to prohibit weapons that result in unnecessary suffering beyond the legitimate goal of war.[35]

The International Red Cross (1870) was organized to mitigate suffering during war. The Hague Conventions (1899, 1907) were also part of a tendency in support of the delimiting ideal of a just war because they sought to impose humanitarian constraints on the conduct of war and not to outlaw war altogether. For example, the 1907 Hague Convention spelled out the following principle: "The right of belligerents to adopt means of injuring the enemy is not unlimited" (Article 22).[36] Although the later Geneva Conventions (1949) have largely replaced them owing to the growth of modern military technology (e.g., the use of submarines, blockade, and aerial bombardment), the Hague Conventions did fix standards in war that would ban *unnecessary* suffering for prisoners and disabled combatants and respect the immunity of civilians and non-military targets (i.e., so-called collateral damage). Weapons with poison gas were outlawed.[37] Further, very important in this regard was the Geneva Protocol on Poison Gas and Bacteriological Warfare (1925), which was an early disavowal of biological and chemical substances as legitimate weapons of war.[38] (However, it is worth noting that nations are still permitted to manufacture and stockpile such weapons for reasons of deterrence.) The Geneva Convention of 1929 was valuable because it provided certain regulations for how prisoners of war should be treated. Finally, the Pact of Paris (1928), or as it is called, the Briand-Kellogg Pact, was the General Treaty for the Renunciation of War. By outlawing, and criminalizing, war as an instrument of national policy, i.e., aggressive (not defensive) war, this treaty became another milestone in the growing body of international law involving the rules of war. Indeed, the IMT in its *Judgment* explicitly affirmed its dependence on many of the afore-mentioned treaties, conventions, and customs.[39]

Individualism, Nationalism, and Globalism

One other aspect of international law, which is a continuing source of conflict, must be addressed because of its impact on the Nuremberg proceedings. It refers, on the one hand, to the tension between an absolutist concept of nonintervention in the internal affairs of a sovereign state while it pursues its own interests as it sees fit, and on the other hand, to the treaties, customs, and so forth of international law and the laws of war and to the criminalization of genocide and the demands of international human rights obligations. The current system of independent nation states is usually understood to have originated in the Treaties of Wesphalia (1648) ending the Thirty Years War. More than a century later, thirteen American colonies declared their independence and freedom from England. The earlier treaties coupled with the adoption by the former colonies of the Articles of Confederation (1777), the Constitution (1787), and the Bill of Rights (1791) gave a great impetus to international law.[40] As noted by one legal authority, these legal instruments had demonstrated how, by common agreement, sovereign states could join in a new and united confederation that could enact laws obligating the whole community and that could protect the rights of citizens by judicial and administrative agencies. Of course, this internationalist trend would subvert the prominent early nineteenth-century Hegelian idea of the (Prussian) state as an independent, irreducible seat of authority. As an aside, the expression "international law" acquired its initial prominence when the philosopher Jeremy Bentham published his famous book in which he preferred this usage of the customary "law of nations."[41] Nevertheless, the body of international law still has within its fold a powerful tension between an individualist concept of the sovereign state and a universalist concept of humanity, the community of nations or "Planethood" (to use B. Ferencz's term).

Prior to certain historical developments in the West in the nineteenth century, it was believed by many people on the grounds of a natural law theory that international law and natural (human) rights carried obligations more fundamental than those imposed by local or lesser political and social institutions. On this theory, all public institutions have legitimacy insofar as they promote or at least conform to moral ideals and principles of justice.[42] According to this conception (of Locke and Grotius), obligations respecting basic rights and justice overrule or limit efforts in fulfillment of more parochial interests. In a sense, this theory anticipated the principles adopted for the Nuremberg trials.

But along with the rise of nationalism and its philosophical underpinnings of absolute sovereignty and noninterference in the unrestricted pursuit of national self-interest (unlike Bentham's utilitarian calculations of individual self-interest, the nation being merely aggregates of individuals) came the inevitable clash with and eclipse of the earlier philosophical doctrine of abstract individual basic rights. In the twentieth century, the evolving and growing body of international law, especially the laws of war, gave substantial and authoritative support to the framers of the Nuremberg Charter and the eventual judgment of the IMT. Once again, the principle of limited sovereignty acquired renewed respectability, which meant that both sovereigns and individual persons may legitimately be held accountable for policies, interests, or actions that either violate the principles and precepts of international law or fail to discharge their supervening obligations to respect law, conscience, and the peaceful resolution of conflicts.

The Nuremberg Charter "defined war crimes as violations of the laws or customs of war."[43] Such crimes as the killing of hostages, though not specifically prohibited by the Fourth Hague Convention nevertheless was deemed "criminal" under international law, on the basis of Grotius's idea of international law and because it is a practice contrary to the laws of humanity.[44]

Also, the moral concept of conscience was said to have been incorporated by the tribunal's judgment, in conjunction with the laws of war, in specifying the "crimes against humanity" committed by the Nazis.

"The only crimes considered by the Tribunal to fall within this category . . . were the murder and ill-treatment of prisoners of war and civilian populations, the pillage of public and private property, slave labor, and racial persecution carried to the point of extermination, all of which had to be committed in connection with or in execution of aggressive war."[45]

In its acceptance of the general notion of "crimes against humanity" as cognizable in international law, the IMT had limited the notion to "principles acceptable to all civilized peoples" and in effect had applied the conscience of humanity to a fact situation.[46] Accordingly, the IMT excluded from its jurisdiction those Nazi crimes that were committed against German Jewish citizens or other civilians prior to the German invasion of Poland (1939), the event that marked the beginning of a "war of aggression," i.e., World War II. However, prior persecutory mistreatment had justiciable importance in demonstrating "conspiracy to wage aggressive war."[47] As a noted legal scholar (and prosecutor at Nuremberg) explains, the reason for this decision about jurisdiction was that if the IMT "had assumed jurisdiction to try persons under international law for crimes committed by them that were not related to war it would have wholly disregarded the concept of sovereignty and subjected to criminal prosecution under international law individuals whose conduct was lawful under controlling municipal law in times of peace."[48] This move gave some recognition to the ancient principle of jurisprudence that "without law, there is no crime." And yet the enormity of Nazi brutality invoked a moral code.

In explicitly recognizing the idea of "crimes against humanity" for the first time in history, the IMT made a significant moral contribution to international law. However, to be actionable in a court of law, such crimes must be committed in execution of other crimes within the jurisdiction of the IMT (e.g., of a "war of aggression"); they do not stand entirely on their own. In short, the signal advancement at Nuremberg centers on holding a country internationally responsible for what it does to its own citizens, not only to other nationals or peoples, regardless of what its own domestic laws allow. Soon thereafter a United Nations resolution explicitly adopted the Nuremberg Charter as international law. The line between international law and morality or justice is not always clearly delineated. In the words of the late U.S. Supreme Court Justice Benjamin Cardozo: "International law . . . has at times, like the common law within states, a twilight existence during which it is hardly distinguishable from morality or justice, till at length the imprimatur of a court attests its jural quality."[49] The philosopher Ralph B. Perry explains the Cardozo phrase "twilight existence" as being "represented by the conscience of the community, speaking for a right."[50]

SOME PHILOSOPHICAL CONSIDERATIONS

In crafting the moral case in Chapter 4 for continuing the prosecution of fugitive Nazi war criminals, I find it necessary to briefly review a number of significant legal-philosophical issues raised before and during the Nuremberg trials. These issues often resurface, for reasons stemming from either ignorance, curiosity, or political motives, as if none had ever been resolved satisfactorily.

Evidently, the impact of these issues may be treated as an impetus to healthy reexamination or else it is calculated to impugn the legitimacy of current prosecutions by vitiating the basis for the original trials. By citing the historical record, as has been abundantly done in the reputable literature, I am hopeful that I can lay to rest at least some of the gnawing questions from well-meaning skeptics.

I will address only those issues whose successful resolution convinced the legal experts that the IMT could be soundly established and that the trials could go forward. Of course, if any of these issues had remained unresolved or answered differently, the trials would have been largely trivialized or invalidated. There were a number of key issues that had to be faced by the policymakers either before or during the London Conference (1945) or by the IMT and the prosecutors at the trials. All were resolved by the policymakers of the Big Four (the United States, Britain, France, and the Soviet Union), though not always unanimously, leading to the adoption of the Charter of the IMT.

The Purpose of the Trials

The first issue involved the central purpose of the trials: Were they to assess the punishment that the accused were to be made to suffer? Or were they to determine the guilt or innocence of the accused?[51] The issue was resolved in favor of the latter. In the words of the charter of the IMT: "The judgment of the Tribunal as to the guilt or the innocence of any Defendant shall give the reasons on which it is based."[52]

Ultimately, three defendants were acquitted. In other words, for the Nuremberg trials to be judicial and not "political" (whereby accusation is tantamount to conviction), the tribunal must lawfully interpret the evidence and thereupon make a judicial finding; it cannot decide beforehand "to ratify a political decision to convict," as Jackson remarked.[53]

The "Only Following Orders" Defense

The second issue was more complex. It was raised both at the London Conference and by the Nazi defense as well during the judicial proceedings. The defense counsel argued that the accused were merely following the orders of their superiors and also that they could not be prosecuted for violating laws that were nonexistent until the charter made their actions illegal—*after* the actions had been committed. The two arguments by the defense are logically related because no action is prima facie excusable if done in obedience to the unlawful or clearly immoral commands of a superior. The Nazis argued, as did the charter's detractors, that the charter *created* law and was not merely restating or applying existing international law. For if, in fact, the charter and the tribunal were based on ex post facto legislation, it would violate a most important Anglo-American constitutional principle that no person shall be deemed punishable "save in accordance with law in effect at the time of his act."[54] This concept is a basic principle of criminal jurisprudence (*nulla poena* or *nullum crimen sine lege*), i.e., no crime has been committed nor is punishment legally enforceable if no valid law exists beforehand that defines certain penalities for actions identified as "criminal." In particular, the issue involved whether initiating and waging a war of aggression is criminal in accordance with international law. Despite some conceptual difficulties in abstractly defining the boundary lines between aggressive and defensive war, the fact situation with respect to the actions of the Nazi leadership was sufficiently unambiguous.

After secretly arming themselves, the German government planned and carried out the occupation of the demilitarized Rhineland (which violated the Versailles and other treaties) in March 1936 in the name of restoring the integrity of German sovereignty; invaded Austria (the *Anschluss*) and annexed part of Czechoslovakia in 1938; invaded and conquered Poland in 1939, an act that the IMT regarded as the start of Germany's war of aggression, and then the Scandinavian countries, Yugoslavia, and Greece. The Germans then proceeded to repudiate the nonaggression pact made with the Soviet Union in 1939 "and without any declaration of war invaded Soviet Territory thereby beginning a War of Aggression against the U.S.S.R."[55] In any case, the representatives at the London Conference, other than the Americans, were satisfied with the judgment that Hitler's aggressions were at least violations of treaties, agreements, and assurances, e.g., the Locarno Treaty of 1925, the Briand-Kellog Pact of 1927–1928 (which renounced war), and others; but the U.S. delegates persuaded them to accept the larger notion of aggressive war.

The IMT (and the Tokyo Tribunal as well) held that the provisions of the charter that declared—not legislated—as criminal the planning and initiating of wars of aggression were grounded in established international law. In addition, the Nazis were shown to have committed atrocities and violations of accepted rules of war that all civilized nations have prohibited in their criminal law.[56] Therefore, in view of international customs, practices, declarations, treaties, and the dictates of modern public or universal conscience, the IMT held that its acknowledged expansion of traditional war crimes to include aggressive war as a "supreme international crime" was not an unprecedented imposition on national sovereignty; rather, it was an overriding requirement of justice in international relations that constrains the conduct of nations in a civilized community of nations. In short, a war of aggression is the most inclusive war crime since it is believed to contain the accumulated evil of all other war crimes.[57] Germany's aggression was "an illegitimate attack on the international peace and order" and was illegal from its beginning.[58]

A Government's Persecution of Its Own Nationals

An important issue regarding whether a government can be prosecuted under international law for committing crimes against its own people was unprecedented before the trials. It has come to be accepted that an advance in international law occurred because of Nuremberg. The IMT held a country internationally responsible for what it did to its own people in carrying out government policy particularly in respect to German Jews, no matter what its own national laws (dis-)allowed, not only what it did to citizens or people of other countries in violation of the customs and laws of war. Moreover, individual members of organizations of a country engaged in a war of aggression were, for the first time, considered by the IMT to be subject to criminal prosecution under international law as set forth in the Nuremberg Charter (which empowered the IMT to make such declarations). Accordingly, the judicial process was enlarged to include all "active" Nazi participants,[59] with the exception of those individuals uninvolved in criminal conduct or uninformed about the criminal activities or purposes of the organization to which they belonged.

The Respondeat Superior Defense and the "Act of State" Doctrine

The defense counsel often argued that the defendants could take refuge in the affirmation that their actions were performed in obedience to the commands of their sovereign leader or superior, i.e., they were simply following orders. Hence they invoked the principle that the master, and not the servant, should be held accountable for prohibited or illicit or criminal acts (i.e., the *respondeat superior* defense). If the evidence by the Nazi defense could show that all commands originated from the Führer (Hitler), the effect would be to deny the prosecution a cause of action or at least excuse or mitigate punishment. In a totalitarian state under Nazi rule, the Führer was the undisputed commander, so all others, some of the defense counsel asserted, were subordinates merely carrying out the sovereign's orders. This reasoning was called the Leadership Principle in Germany: the führer (leader) assumes all powers *and* all responsibility.[60] A related principle that the Nuremberg Charter minimized or rejected as a possible defense was that the officials of the government would be protected because their orders and acts were essentially official acts of state, which legally would free them from criminal responsibility. The Act of State Doctrine, as a matter of U.S. law (but not necessarily recognized in international law), provided that "the courts of one country will not sit in judgment on the acts of the government of another, done within its own territory."[61] In any case, the charter of the IMT provided, in anticipation of defense arguments about the twin principles of *respondeat superior* and Act of State immunity, that the "official position of defendants, whether as Heads of State or responsible officials in Government Departments, shall not be considered as freeing them from responsibility or mitigating punishment." Also, the "fact that [an individual] acted pursuant to [superior orders] shall not free him from responsibility, but may be considered in mitigation of punishment."[62] On the authority of the charter, rooted as it was in common law and established international law, Justice Jackson and the prosecution regarded these defense pleas as void of legal validity and evasions of personal responsibility. The plea that "following orders" was a coerced act, i.e., the actor had no other choice but to obey the superior's command under threat of serious penalty for disobedience, was rejected as well. For the prosecution pointed out that the defendants had helped to bring Hitler to power in Germany and then knowledgeably cooperated with him in the realization of his intentions. None resigned. Protests were few and far between to Hitler's reign of terror. Jackson noted that at least one German general had a father who left the Nazis and retired in 1941.

Defendant Admiral Erich Raeder conceded that he had the option to resign. A few other defendants had relinquished certain duties or offices every so often.[63] Consequently, a moral option was possible, and so coercion is an inappropriate description of the role and actions played by the defendants. In response to the defense plea of ignorance about the bigger picture of criminality in which the defendants were engaged, a leading British prosecutor asked how anyone could accept the proposition

> that a man who was either a minister or a leading executive in a state that, within the space of six years, transported seven million men, women and children for labor, exterminated 275,000 of its own aged and mentally infirm, and annihilated in the gas chambers or by shooting what must at the lowest computation be twelve million people, remained ignorant of or irresponsible for these crimes?[64]

The "Fairness of the Trials" Issue

The policymakers of the war crimes trials and eventually, too, the tribunal and the prosecutors had to grapple with the unavoidable question about the inherent "fairness" of the trials as it was the victorious allies who were trying the losers, and any putative war crimes committed by the winners would be ignored or downplayed. Also, "fairness" could be calibrated in terms of the procedures in place in the conduct of the trials.

The prosecutors distinguished between the supposedly small number of Allied war crimes that resulted from combat and the unthinkably immense scale of Nazi atrocities. But the distinction was made not in terms of dimension alone; rather, the claim centered on the intent of the Nazis. The chief British prosecutor observed that "the defendants were guilty not of random acts but of 'systematic, wholesale, consistent action taken as a matter of deliberate calculation.'"[65] In response to a defense counsel's argument that what the evidence revealed was not a conspiracy but rather that a number of individuals and institutions in Germany were constantly at odds, Justice Jackson countered that such personal rivalries and conflict were about methods. The intent was shared by all defendants.[66] In most systems of criminal law, an illegal act resulting from intention to commit a crime receives greater legal weight than a similar unpremeditated crime.

How "fair" were the Nuremberg trials? The charter of the IMT contained a set of provisions that entitled individuals who were accused of committing crimes under international law to a trial that was fair. Accordingly, the accused were to be presumed innocent unless evidence adduced at trial established guilt "beyond a reasonable doubt" (a standard rooted in Anglo-American criminal law). All defendants were entitled to receive a full detailed indictment, listing the specifics of the charges against them. They were entitled to present their own defense or have help from legal counsel, including the right to cross-examine witnesses, before or during the proceedings. Moreover, to ensure fairness, the defendants had the right to have the proceedings and other pertinent documents translated into a language they could comprehend.[67] Indeed, a few of the defendants' lawyers later testified in writing to the fairness of both the procedures of the trials and the overall proceedings.[68] Some members of the defense counsel performed brilliantly, seriously, and with a passion for fairness.[69] To the extent that the rights of the defendants were respected (including the right to a complete and appropriate defense) and that the finding of guilt was based on sufficient evidence, according to law, it would be unreasonable to claim that the Nuremberg trials were anything but fair.

The Question of "Victor's Justice"

But for some the question of "victor's justice" may persist, to which the following response, made by the Pulitzer Prize–winning philosopher, R. B. Perry, must be given:

> Had those responsible for the aggressions and inhumanities of the Nazi regime been allowed to go unpunished, mankind would have lost a supreme opportunity to crystallize in legal form a recognized and pressing moral necessity. The time was ripe to step across the line from conscience to a legal order, and to create a legal precedent for future time. Those who would have preferred exoneration, or assassination, or summary execution, were not the friends of law in principle, but the defenders of outmoded law or of the perpetuation of lawlessness.[70]

The "moral necessity" of which Perry has written cannot be summarily dismissed as mere "victor's justice." In my view, this pejorative veneer will dissipate only as the historical record of the Nuremberg trials is fully understood.

The common nuance carried by the expression "victor's justice" is that it is a misnomer, a linguistic cover-up for the certain process by which a victor imposes its will on the vanquished. Prior to the Nuremberg trials, it was known as executive or administrative action because the losing party was punished without due process of law. Of course, in an unintended miscarriage of justice, the victorious nation might mistakenly bring innocent parties from the losing side to trial and wrongly convict them. But it seems self-defeating to put those accused of war crimes through a judicial process only to undermine one's own credibility in the eyes of the community of nations and international law by declarations of unproven guilt and summary punishment (not unlike the German courts under Nazi rule, which became mere enforcers of Hitler's fiats).[71] Therefore, the inevitable power victorious nations have over defeated nations need not degenerate into "victor's justice," as I believe the legacy of the Nuremberg trials demonstrates. It is no argument to claim, as alternate IMT Judge John J. Parker observed, that if the Nazis had been victorious they would not have had to suffer the war crimes trials since, by winning, they would have placed themselves "beyond the reach of justice" or prosecution for their wrongdoings.[72] It is evident that the Nazi offenders deserved to be punished for their crimes; fortunately, the victors had the power, will, and expertise to prosecute them in accordance with the evolving rule of law.

This second meaning conveyed by the term "victor's justice" connotes the attempt by the victor to institute a scheme of justice by which the actions, policies, and participants of the losing side may be judged.

Although the Nuremberg trials may wrongly be seen as an occasion for the victor to camouflage retributive vengeance, they were in fact used to crystallize a set of legal and moral standards. Hence the standards that emerged as a basis for the trials were not merely ex post facto having no "jural quality," despite appearances, but rather were "generated from custom or conscience by application to cases deemed of sufficient importance to warrant the intervention of society as a whole."[73] Again, these standards are the laws against genocide and against wars of aggression and the laws that promote peaceful and humane relations among nations. Moreover, the Nuremberg trials represent the elevation of the rule of law over the rule of force. In a sense, this issue appears trivial because conquerors always are expected realistically to wield power—to dominate and bend the conquered to their will. The nontrivial and more interesting sense of "victor's justice," to which I have alluded, refers to an exercise of the rule of law in accordance with a higher responsibility incumbent on a law-respecting victor to secure a rights-respecting, democratically inspired world based on the ideals of law, morality, and justice. However, some still rightly question whether the principles recognized at Nuremberg have been realized and enforced, not by power of arms but prior to armed victory in the form of global institutions such as an international court of criminal justice with compulsory and universal jurisdiction.[74]

NOTES

1. Ann Tusa and John Tusa, *The Nuremberg Trial* (New York: Athenium, 1984), pp. 24–31.

2. Marian Mushkat, "Nuremberg Trial," in Israel Gutman, ed., *Encyclopedia of the Holocaust*, vol. 4 (New York: Macmillan, 1990), pp. 1489–90. See also Telford Taylor, *The Anatomy of the Nuremberg Trials* (New York: Knopf, 1992), pp. 618–27, passim.

3. The SS was Hitler's elite guard; it controlled police, concentration camps, and killing functions. The Sicherheitsdienst was the secret security or intelligence branch of the SS. The Geheime Staats Polizei (the Gestapo) was the Secret State Police. The SS also included the infamous extermination squads known as the Einsatzaruppen; see Ronald Headland, *Messages of Murder* (Cranbury: Associated University Presses, 1992), for extensive details about reports of these mobile killing units of the SS.

4. Henry T. King, Jr., "Nuremberg Revisited," *Gamut*, no. 7 (Fall 1982), p. 57.

5. Priscilla Dale Jones, "General Survey," *Encyclopedia of the Holocaust*, pp. 1488–89.

6. Whitney Harris, "Justice Jackson at Nuremberg," *International Lawyer*, vol. 20, no. 3 (Summer 1986), p. 870.

7. Robert H. Jackson, in an address to the American Society of International Law, cited by Harris, "Justice Jackson at Nuremberg," p. 869.

8. Ingrid Detter De Lupis, *The Law of War* (Cambridge: Cambridge University Press, 1987), pp. 352–53; also, Steven Fogelson, "The Nuremberg Legacy: An Unfulfilled Promise," *Southern California Law Review*, vol. 63 (March 1990), p. 858.

9. Tusa and Tusa, *Nuremberg Trial*, p. 19.

10. Telford Taylor, *Nuremberg and Vietnam* (Chicago: Quadrangle Books, 1970), pp. 26–27, 78–79. General Taylor was chief U.S. counsel for the prosecution in the Subsequent Trials, the Medical Case.

11. Quoted in Richard A. Falk, Gabriel Kolko, and Robert Jay Lifton, eds., *Crimes of War* (New York: Vintage Books, 1971), pp. 107–08.

12. This analysis was given by Charles Horsky, as I understood him, at a reunion of the Nuremberg prosecution staff in Washington, D.C., March 22–24, 1991, to which I was invited. Horsky would probably be the person who would set up such a tribunal.

13. For specifics relating to each charge, see Robert E. Conot, *Justice at Nuremberg* (New York: Harper and Row, 1983), p. 73; especially Article 6 of the Charter, in Bradley F. Smith, *The American Road to Nuremberg: The Documentary Records 1944–1945* (Stanford: Hoover Institution Press, 1982), p. 215.

14. Cited in Deborah E. Lipstadt, *Beyond Belief* (New York: Free Press, 1986), p. 157; also, see David S. Wyman, *The Abandonment of the Jews* (New York: Pantheon, 1985), pp. 19–41.

15. Lipstadt, *Beyond Belief*, p. 192.

16. Wyman, *Abandonment of the Jews*, pp. 322–27.

17. Lipstadt, *Beyond Belief*, p. 163.

18. Ibid., pp. 163–64.

19. Ibid., pp. 180, 186.

20. Ibid., pp. 191–92.

21. Wyman, *Abandonment of the Jews*, p. xiv; also, see Roosevelt's statement on German war crimes, 1944, in Falk et al., *Crimes of War*, pp. 76–77.

22. Conot, *Justice at Nuremberg*, p. 518.

23. Quoted in George Seldes, *The Great Thoughts* (New York: Ballantine Books, 1985), p. 80.

24. Detter De Lupis, *Law of War*, p. 24.

25. See Hugo Grotius, *The Law of War and Peace* (1625), trans. William Whewell (Cambridge: Cambridge University Press, 1853); Emrich de Vattel, *The Law of Nations* (1758), 3 vols., trans. Charles G. Fenwick (Washington, D.C.: Carnegie Institution, 1916).

26. Taylor, *Nuremberg and Vietnam*, p. 19.

27. Detter De Lupis, *Law of War*, pp. 121–22, 122, n. 9.

28. Ibid.

29. Baron de Montesquieu, *The Spirit of the Laws* (New York: Hafner Press, 1949), pp. 134, 137, 135, respectively.

30. Quoted in Ian Clark, *Waging War* (Oxford: Clarendon Press, 1990), p. 55.

31. Detter De Lupis, *Law of War*, p. 123.

32. Quoted in ibid., p. 123, n. 19.

33. *Black's Law Dictionary*, 5th ed. (St. Paul: West, 1979), pp. 368, 1076.

34. Thomas Buergenthal and Harold G. Maier, *Public International Law* (St. Paul: West, 1990), pp. 172–73.

35. Quoted in Falk et al., *Crimes of War*, pp. 31–32.

36. Taylor, *Nuremberg and Vietnam*, p. 22.

37. Falk et al., *Crimes of War*, p. 33.

38. Ibid., p. 43.

39. Fogelson, "Nuremberg Legacy" p. 861; also, Whitney R. Harris, *Tyranny on Trial* (Dallas: Southern Methodist University Press, 1970), p. 505. Harris was a prominent member of the U.S. prosecution at Nuremberg.

40. Benjamin Ferencz, *A Common Sense Guide to World Peace* (New York: Oceana Publications, 1985), p. 3; Ferencz was chief U.S. prosecutor in the Nuremberg war crimes trial against German murder squads that had exterminated over 1 million innocent people. The Associated Press called this trial "the biggest murder trial in history."

41. Jeremy Bentham, *The Principles of Morals and Legislation* (1789) (New York: Hafner, 1948), pp. 326–27.

42. Kent Greenawalt, *Conflicts of Law and Morality* (New York: Oxford University Press, 1989), pp. 58, 161–68, 186–94.

43. Harris, *Tyranny on Trial*, p. 507.

44. Ibid., p. 508.

45. Ibid., pp. 511, 513.

46. Ibid., p. 511.

47. Ibid., p. 512.

48. Ibid., p. 512.

49. Quoted by Ralph Barton Perry, *Realms of Value* (Cambridge: Harvard University Press, 1968), p. 245.

50. Ibid., p. 245.

51. Harris, "Justice Jackson at Nuremberg," p. 871.

52. Article 26. The Charter is reprinted in Bradley F. Smith, *American Road to Nuremberg*, p. 219.

53. Harris, "Justice Jackson at Nuremberg," p. 872.

54. Harris, *Tyranny on Trial*, p. 517.

55. Eugene Davidson *The Trial of the Germans* (New York: Collier Books, 1966), p. 23.

56. Smith, *American Road to Nuremberg*, p. 85.

57. Harris, "Justice Jackson at Nuremberg," p. 873.

58. *Report of Robert H. Jackson, United States Representative to the International Conference on Military Trials*, U.S. Department of State Publication no. 3080, pp. 383–84 (1949).

59. Harris, "Justice Jackson at Nuremberg," pp. 875–76.

60. Tusa and Tusa, *Nuremberg Trial*, p. 416.

61. Quoted in Fogelson, "Nuremberg Legacy," p. 865.

62. Articles 7 and 8, respectively, in Smith, *American Road to Nuremberg*, p. 215–16; from the Charter.

63. From the Proceedings IX and XIV, quoted in John A. Appleman, *Military Tribunals and International Crimes* (Westport: Greenwood Press, 1971), p. 56.

64. The words of Sir Hartley Shawcross, quoted in Tusa and Tusa, *Nuremberg Trial*, pp. 419–20.

65. Ibid., p. 420.

66. Ibid.

67. The Charter of the IMT, IV, Articles 16a, b, c, d, e; in Smith, *American Road to Nuremberg*, pp. 217–18.

68. In Fogelson, "Nuremberg Legacy," p. 860; cited were Carl Haensel, "The Nuremberg Trial Revisited," *De Paul Law Review*, vol. 13 (1964), pp. 248, 258; Otto Pannenbecker, "The Nuremberg War-Crimes Trial," *De Paul Law Review*, vol. 14 (1965), pp. 348, 350, 356.

69. Appleman, *Military Tribunals*, p. 345.

70. Perry, *Realms of Value*, p. 246.

71. See Case no. 3, the Justice Case, at Nuremberg, in Appleman, *Military Tribunals*, pp. 157–62.

72. John J. Parker, "International Trial at Nuremberg: Giving Vitality to International Law," *American Bar Association Journal*, vol. 37 (1951), p. 552.

73. Perry, *Realms of Value*, p. 245.

74. Fogelson, "Nuremberg Legacy"; also, Henry T. King, Jr. "Towards the Humanization of Technology," *Case Western Reserve Law Review*, vol. 19, no. 1 (November 1967), p. 129; H. King was a former U.S. prosecutor at Nuremberg, specifically in the Milch case. Erhard Milch was charged with the exploitation of slave labor and responsibility for some German air force–related medical experiments on inmates of concentration camps. Milch was convicted.

4

THE RULE OF LAW

Defendants are charged with crimes of such immensity that mere specific instances of criminality appear insignificant by comparison. The charge, in brief, is that of conscious participation in a nationwide government-organized system of cruelty and injustice, in violation of the laws of war and of humanity, and perpetrated in the name of law by the authority of the Ministry of Justice, and through the instrumentality of the courts. The dagger of the assassin was concealed beneath the robe of the jurist.

—The International Military Tribunal's conclusion

In this chapter, the concept of the rule of law will be characterized in a fashion that lends support to my case for sustaining efforts to prosecute the remaining Nazi offenders almost half a century later.[1] To discuss this issue profitably, we must appreciate the roles played by law and morality in our contemporary vision of a liberal constitutional democracy. In my opinion, we may recognize in the moral and legal legacy of the Nuremberg trials a special exhibition of the interplay among the laws of war, treaties, the common law, and conscience. The victorious nations were spurred by both moral necessity and political opportunity to respond to the pervasive atrocities of the Nazi regime. Their response was framed largely on the basis of a landmark multinational conception of the rule of law.

Historically, the fusion of politics, morality, and law is expressed in the American idea of constitutionalism, which arose partly in the struggles against absolutist and arbitrary political rule. The phrase 'rule of law' as I intend it in this context refers not only to the trilogy of essentials—codes, courts, and enforcement—but also to the subordination of political governance, in both substance and process, to the basic 'law of the land.' For instance, the Constitution of the United States of America as the embodiment of this basic law defines the establishment, purpose, and proper function of government respecting the diffusion and limits of governmental powers and the protection of the fundamental moral, political, and legal rights of persons to live in peace and dignity in society.[2] In the latter case, the liberal ideal of the rule of law refers to a (jural) social institution by which individual citizens are at least left free to live their own lives in fulfillment of their self-chosen life plans, provided that they respect the same basic rights of others and society's laws, but also expect to suffer a prescribed and proportionate penalty on conviction by an authorized judicial body for serious wrongdoing.

A contrasting idea might propose a constitution as a 'basic law' to be used by the supreme or sovereign political power in dealings with citizens, when it serves its purpose to do so, but where the sovereign political power itself is not strictly bound by the letter or spirit of its provisions. Soviet law has in the past functioned in this way. This idea was even more nearly true of the Nazi judicial system, with the arguable exception to this idea that the Nazi leader, the Führer, did not derive his power from constitutional authority, since, as some experts have held, German law was superseded by the Hitlerian dictatorship.[3] This question at one time became a hotly contested issue about the validity of Nazi "laws." I will discuss this issue as it was argued by two prominent legal theorists because it will illumine how in the extreme a government's contempt for the normative purpose of the law can destroy a legal system.

In any case, mention of this issue invites an observation about scholarship that has complicated, even blurred, the outlines of the issue. For if published documentation in the 1980s shows that the postwar efforts at denazifying (or reeducating or even reorientating Germany) were largely unsuccessful,[4] the continuity of antidemocratic ideology, laws, institutions, and professional legal personnel between pre-Hitlerite Germany and the Nazi and post-Nazi years has been generally undervalued, particularly for its impact on the "validity of Nazi law" issue. It may not be nearly so easy to distinguish valid from invalid law in the history of the German legal system, particularly in light of the subtleties of lawmaking and their relation to universal moral standards. The nazified interpretive subtext of judicial decisionmaking miscarried legal justice in Nazi Germany as surely as explicitly stated Nazi legislation did.

In a world with a large and diverse plurality of institutional arrangements about the proper place and purpose of law,[5] failure to incorporate or respect basic human rights in a nation's constitution will stigmatize a society today and raise the specter of its government's illegitimacy. At the same time, the philosophical constraints imposed by the Western liberal idea of the rule of law need not be an insurmountable hindrance to a cohesive internationalization of law nor to multilateral agreements about what the law is, by and to whom it is to be applied, and toward what end(s). After all, this concept is what the measured success of the Nuremberg trials has taught us. Like a domestic legal system, international law also functions routinely in matters of commerce and multinational corporate enterprise, communication, transportation, and diplomatic relations,[6] notwithstanding the United Nations Charter provision involving the priority of "domestic jurisdiction" and its correlative principle of nonintervention.[7] My point is that the legal and political particularities of the world's nations may be subordinated to higher international standards and interests, e.g., in agreements to resolve conflicts peacefully or to bring future war criminals to justice.

Anglo-American law has strongly influenced the form, direction, and importance of international law with respect to the conception of basic rights of individuals, peoples, and nations in a world community (also, American legal expertise has been sought by constitution-makers in a large number of nations).[8] Under this influence, these rights may also be expressed in the language of standards or moral ideals such as a protected sphere of personal freedom and privacy, universal moral and legal equality, popular political sovereignty and control. Accordingly, we note the righteous indignation we are likely to feel when we believe that these standards are violated or are in some way unmet; the defense or burden of justification always falls on those who are responsible for or who have committed the offense. No legitimate or rational democratic scheme of governance today will find refuge from criticism about its legitimacy if its policies or rules are arbitrary or are carried into effect arbitrarily by unfairly or wrongly disadvantaging some of its citizens in their relations with other citizens in terms of basic rights and obligations.

CHARACTERISTICS OF LAW UNDER NAZI RULE

A brief look at some characteristic Nazi legislation, institutions, legal concepts, practices, and professional legal personnel offers a paradigm case about how the rule of law can be destroyed, leaving only a veneer of legal form and process. In addition, critics of the idea of 'rule of law,' as I have construed it, will not find relief in the argument from ethnocentrism that the substantial differences between German and U.S. law remain unacknowledged and not only account for some of the obvious perversions of justice under Nazi rule but also require an appraisal only by internal "German" standards (i.e., right-wing conservatives and sympathetic Nazis). I will address this criticism (which I believe to be groundless) in the context of the philosophical debate about the validity of Nazi law only after I present a sketch of law under the Nazi regime.

The prominence of Carl Schmitt, the self-styled constitutional theorist of the Third Reich, had promoted the respectability of his old "friend or foe" doctrine as it was formally described in his book, *The Concept of the Political* (1927). The common distinction in European countries between 'legal opposition' and treason was collapsed into the distinction between virtual unqualified loyalty to the interests and leadership of the state, on the one hand, or treason, on the other. Thus Schmitt's famous doctrine of the "national emergency" where the state is threatened by "enemies from within" (note the application of the "friend or foe" doctrine) was utilized by the Nazis to justify whatever was needed to accomplish their ends. For example, the emergency enabling act of 1933, officially called the Law to Remove the Danger to the People and the Reich, afforded Hitler the power to rule by decree. And rule by decree he and other leading Nazis did, sorting out friend from foe as they went along and setting up a nationwide judicial apparatus that would deal with the enemies of the Reich under legal cover.

(Even Schmitt himself personalized the distinction by rejecting his former Jewish friends in a surge of antisemitism.)[9] The basic legal principle of Nazi rule: "Whatever benefits the People is right." In fact, this principle was accepted by Germany's courts a number of years before the Nazis came to power.[10] Sadly, the German legal system, dominated by doctrinaire conservative German nationalists both in the decade before and during the Nazi regime, gradually supported accused criminals who acted from patriotic German motives, even if they were not German. This was certainly true of Hitler's trial after the Beer Hall Putsch (1923), for the judges merely ignored the deportation rule in his case (Hitler was Austrian). They claimed he was a patriotic German in spirit.[11] Eventually, the German Supreme Court's recognition of the "defense of the state" doctrine as a warrant for murder would undermine the integrity of the legal system itself.[12]

In placing the state and its defense above the law, a noted expert explains, the highest German court was purveying a "fatal message": that "the most heinous crimes were not punishable if they were committed in the interest of the state, while legal actions were punishable if they ran counter to it."[13]

The Decree for the Protection of the People (the "Reichstag Fire" Decree) simply annulled most civil rights guaranteed under the Weimar Constitution, and other decrees were issued mandating the death penalty for acts of arson and for such "treasonable" activities as the spreading of "rumors or false reports," strikes, publications, or rallies against Nazis.[14] The infamous Nuremberg race laws were passed mainly for the purpose of isolating the Jewish population from the body of German citizenry. Not only had legislators presumed to define who was a Jew, they used personal identification and bioracial criteria for making the discrimination. These laws were an instance of unveiled dominative power and gave putative legal standing to the spurious but pervasive notion of the bioracial health of the so-called Aryan German community by arbitrarily excluding Jewish citizens from exercising any legal rights enjoyed by other, favored citizens of the Reich.[15] Such laws as the Law for the Protection of German Blood and German Honor, the defense laws, the Law for the Restoration of the Professional Civil Service, the Reich citizenship law, all passed by 1935, exemplify the Nazi legislative assault on the legal and moral rights of German Jews.[16]

As an example, Nazi judges facilitated the divorce process by awarding so-called Aryan spouses the legal "right to divorce their racially undesirable partners without proving guilt."[17] By 1938, judicial decisions included the following among the grounds for divorce: "adultery, refusal to procreate . . . racial incompatibility, and eugenic weakness."[18] Hitler's Night and Fog Decree (December 7, 1941) ordered the death penalty for any persons who endangered the security or preparedness of the Nazi-sympathetic regimes in the occupied territories. In addition, the accused would often in fact disappear, and their fate would remain unpublicized.[19]

Nazi Courts

In the 1930s, the jurists "coordinated" themselves by issuing a decree that called for the removal of all judges who were either Jewish, Democratist, or "politically unreliable."[20] Those judges who remained expressed their willingness to decide cases in favor of the compelling interests of the Nazi leadership of the Third Reich. By the mid-1930s, over one-third of the country's law professors had been dismissed for reasons of race or politics.[21] By 1939, at least two-thirds of the law faculty had been appointed after the Nazis came to power; eventually, their most compliant students assumed positions of judicial and legislative authority in the Federal Republic after the Allies' destruction of Nazi rule.

The Reich Ministry of Justice, the prosecution staff at the national level, and special military and civilian courts were convened both within Germany and in its occupied countries and territories in order to realize Nazi goals.[22] Of special note were the Special Panel of the Supreme Court and the infamous People's Court, created in 1933 and 1934, respectively. Their task: to obliterate the enemies of the Reich under the guise of judicial process and to intimidate the general public. The most well-known proceeding of the latter court was the trial of the conspirators involved in the failed attempt to assassinate Hitler in 1944. Their speedy conviction was a foregone conclusion. They were executed within hours after the verdict, the appeals process for "disloyal" defendants long having been curtailed. Guilt by association resulted in the arrests and placement in concentration camps for hundreds of friends and relatives of the coconspirators.[23] The jurisdiction of the People's Court had gradually expanded from cases involving treason and attacks on the property or leadership of the Reich (which had heretofore come before the Supreme

Court) to those involving any subversion of the "will of the Führer." A
lesser-known case concerned Hans and Sophie Scholl, leading members
of the small and heroic White Rose Resistance group. They were prosecuted and executed on order of the People's Court for the capital crime
of distributing anti-Nazi pamphlets at a university,[24] and so was their
mentor, a philosophy professor (Kurt Huber).[25] The well-known German
military man, Field Marshall Erwin Rommel (of the Africa Corps) was to
be charged with treason and prosecuted before the People's Court. He
chose instead to die by his own hand.[26]

In both substance, process, and consequence, the impact of the Nazi
"judicial" process could not support respect for the rule of law but rather
quickened fear of running afoul of the certified ideology and authority. In
addition, it deprived Jews and other unfortunate people of all rights (and
protections) of citizenship and personhood. The People's Court was a
legal tool of Nazi terror because it degraded any claim to judicial impar-
tiality and fairness; it placed on trial and executed almost immediately
over 5,000 people whom it judged (seemingly beforehand) to be enemies
of the Nazi state. Its proceedings were customarily held in camera (like
England's Star Chamber, also unaccountable), and no appeal of its sentences was permitted.[27] Defense lawyers were typically also committed
Nazis. For example, as already noted, the People's Court was used to try
and to convict some 200 people implicated in a plot to assassinate Hitler.
Most were executed within hours of being sentenced. Appeals were
pointless.[28] These special courts, apparently consistent with legal proceedings in other German courts, "were not subject to the usual rules.
And, under the doctrines of 'analogy' and the 'sound feelings of the
people,' it was not necessary for a conviction that a person even have
violated an existing law."[29]

Eventually, many of Germany's chief justices, prosecutors, and some
leading officials of the Justice Ministry under Nazi rule were put on trial
in the subsequent Nuremberg Proceedings (Case No. 3, The Justice
Case).[30] They were charged with war crimes, crimes against humanity,
and membership in a criminal organization (the SS).

Legal Innovations Under Nazi Law

Among the Nazis' legal innovations I include the distorted use of legal
analogy against defendants. The accepted use of legal analogy, governed
by the principle that "like cases should be treated alike," is to compare
two distinct cases in terms of their relevant similarities (I assume that an
analogy is a comparison between two objects or sets of objects that are
similar in some respects, dissimilar in others). Thus Nazi judges used
"analogy" to lump together cases not covered by the plain-text meaning

of the term where the relevant dissimilarities between the cases outweighed the relevant similarities—i.e., judicial decisions were supported by an interpretation inimical to the given law that presumably was too narrow to include the cases the judges sought to try.[31] In these cases, penalties were imposed by analogy. In addition, the teleological method of interpretation facilitated the judicial misuse of analogy by categorizing cases in terms of an interpretation of the aims of the Nazi Reich often in violation of the law.[32] Judges were exhorted to "approach a case with 'healthy prejudice' and 'make value judgments which correspond to the National Socialist legal order and the will of the political leadership.'"[33]

Police agencies also eroded the autonomy and jurisdiction of traditional courts with intensive use of preventive detention, a form of punishment that may be justified, if ever, only under conditions of strict emergency, which was certainly not the case in Nazi Germany. The Nazis made abundant use of retroactive punishment for behavior that was not legally prohibited at the time it was done. Again, the right of appeal of defendants who were presumed by authorities to be "disloyal" was curtailed; some decisions "could be appealed if lodged on behalf of the Führer." These appeals often resulted in the setting aside by a special appeals court (usually the Supreme Court) of a "legal" verdict by grant of a "plea of nullity" and the returning of the case to a lower court for reconsideration along lines of the requirements of a National Socialist order.[34]

In other words, the source of law was no longer "law" in the traditional usage (including statutes, precedents, and sound moral and legal principles). The notorious comment made by Joseph Goebbels (the Nazi propaganda minister) about what Nazism must do may be cited: It must "erase the year 1789 from German history . . . repudiating basic human rights, individual rights vis-à-vis the state, . . . restraints on the state's right to impose punishment" and increasing the powers of the state.[35] The German legal system under Nazism destroyed the vestiges of a just rule of law, in spite of the fact that, as has been generally observed, Germany's commercial, civil, and criminal codes usually remained separate from National Socialist statutes. Nevertheless, the courts were inclined to integrate Nazi legislation with the extant codes in practice.

NAZI JUSTICE: PHILOSOPHICAL PERSPECTIVES

I shall now join the above characterization of the German legal system under Nazi rule with a discussion about its proper place in philosophical perspective.

A famous 'natural law' theorist, Lon Fuller, presented a persuasive critique of legal positivism (e.g., that of H.L.A. Hart) and, more generally, of the abuse of law that occurred in Nazi Germany.[36] My subsequent comments about Fuller are meant to support my idea of the 'rule of law,' so I will circumvent the subtleties involved in Hart's own defense of his positivist theory, which insists on salvaging the thesis of the separation of law and morality (i.e., unjust or immoral law does not invalidate law for that reason).[37] For Fuller, at issue is the matter of the proper conceptual relationship between a system of law and moral principles. The Nazis' perversions of law, both in promulgation and administration, pressed the issue about whether unjust or flagrantly evil 'law' is truly valid (i.e., binding) law. He argues that the nazification of Germany's legal system ultimately invalidated its institutions and rules.[38]

The resolution of this issue in Fuller's case (as in Hart's) depends on how the role of morality is characterized in the formation and endorsement of law. The acquiescence of most of Germany's legal profession (like its medical profession) under Nazi rule was a disgrace, because the Nazis used a "legal" cover to justify their tyranny and repression. In my opinion, this approach to law vitiates respect for law in general, if not for the body of law itself.

Fuller cites the case of a German legal theorist (Gustav Radbruch) who rejected his own earlier, prewar positivism because he blamed Nazi legislation as being the outcome of lawmaking in the absence of respect for basic moral principles (again, the separation of law and morality). In an article cited by Fuller, Radbruch mentioned how, by a secret enactment, the Nazis claimed to legalize the exterminative activities carried on in the concentration camps.[39] Fuller, like Radbruch, came to question whether law that was unpublicized (i.e., secret) or deeply offensive could be called "law." Radbruch is said to have declared that even "legality" itself must respect the "principles of humanitarian morality."[40] In Fuller's view, there are definite "implicit laws of lawmaking" or "canons of internal morality" connected with lawmaking that the Nazis disregarded, to the discredit of the "legal" quality of Nazi legislation. These constraining moral conditions of lawmaking are nowhere in evidence, Fuller testifies, in the case of special Nazi criminal, military, and People's courts. Defendants, accused of treason, were brought before these courts and were typically convicted by accusation alone with minimal or no show of judicial process, sometimes even in violation of the Nazis' own self-proclaimed procedures. Accordingly, it was futile for citizens to examine Nazi law to discern the nature of their legal obligations, since some apparent laws contradicted others. Also, as some laws were unpublicized, or "secret," citizens could not always know what behavior was permissible or prohibited.

Another egregious illustration of the Nazi abuse of lawmaking power concerns, as I have noted, the unjust retroactivity of certain laws. For example, Ernst Röhm and about seventy other members of the SA, a dissident Nazi group, were summarily murdered in Munich in 1934 by Hitler's forces. Hitler, as Führer, arrogated to himself the highest law-making authority in the Third Reich and in this self-appointed capacity decreed that retrospectively these murders—carried out without judicial process—were transformed into legalized executions. Fuller denounces such retroactive legislation as an offense both to justice and to the "implicit demands of legal decency."[41] In fact, Fuller identifies at least eight conditions (or standards) for lawmaking that respect decency, security, and justice in ways that allow citizens to fashion their own lawful conduct, unlike the Nazis, who abused the law by terrorizing citizens into impotence or fearful submission. These conditions include the necessity for government to publicize laws, to make laws clear and understandable, to make laws general (and to avoid decisionmaking on an ad hoc basis), to make laws prospective (not retroactive), to make laws requiring behavior within the control of the citizens affected, and so on.[42]

MORALITY AND NAZI LAW

My own appraisal of this still interesting dispute, briefly stated, is that neither Radbruch, Hart, nor Fuller is entirely correct in his understanding of Nazi "morality" but that each has, in his own respective position, captured some limited "truth." Radbruch is correct for blaming the Nazis for flagrantly disregarding morality in their administrative, legislative, and judicial activities. The complicity of the legal profession (with minimal or no protest) in the unparalleled evil of the Holocaust provides ample testimony for Radbruch's concern about how legal positivism (and its leading doctrine of the separation between law and morality) may have encouraged Nazi lawmaking. But, of course, other factors were most important.[43]

Hart is also correct, in my opinion, when he observes that law, like morality, is very complex and diverse, so that no exhaustive set of a community's (moral) values can be consistently and cohesively absorbed or respected by a single legal system, nor should it be, since law would then lose its authority and integrity if any or all moral standards (some of which surely conflict) were to be applied directly in fixing the legal character of any practice, rule, or principle.

And Fuller, too, is correct in a sense when he ascribes a certain inherent moral quality to a society's institution of law, because if a people could not square its profoundest moral sentiments and values with a society's legal system, the obligatoriness of law would dissipate or lose its essential hold on right-thinking citizens or else dissolve into impotent submission from mere fear of punishment for illegal conduct. (Even most thieves would probably not contest the wrongness of their actions, while expressing the need for rationalizing them, and yet they would opt for the illegal actions anyway for some expected gain they may value.)

In light of this discussion, my own view is that a primary problem with characterizing Nazi rule is not that it was bereft of all moral values (though many individuals in the Third Reich surely were). Instead, the Nazi propagandists were careful to denounce or reject certain moral values and to dramatize and underscore their preference for other "moral" values.[44] For example, Nazi philosopher Walther Darrè is reported to have reformulated I. Kant's famous ethical categorical imperative as follows: "As a German, always act so that your German co-nationals could make you their paragon."[45] Kant's original articulation of this principle was intended to apply universally with respect to all rational (not merely German) beings. It states: "Act only on that maxim through which you can at the same time will that it should become a universal law."[46] What counts here is what meaning its interpreters pack into the term "German." For Kant, moral goodness accrues to actions that respect the categorical imperative.

For the Nazi ideologies, goodness belongs to the racial blood of the Germanic stock. The "prophet laureate" of Nazism, A. Rosenberg (who was convicted at Nuremberg and hanged for his crimes against humanity), published a book called *The Myth of the Twentieth Century.* It was "one of the two great unread bestsellers of the Third Reich."[47] Rosenberg's writing stressed the "conflict of values" necessitated by his "racial interpretation of history."[48] He writes:

> Liberalism preached: Freedom, generosity, freedom of trade, Parliamentarianism, emancipation of women, equality of mankind, equality of sexes, etc., that is to say, it sinned against a law of nature that creative actions can only come from the working of polarized potentials, that a potential energy is necessary . . . to create culture. The German idea today demands in the midst of the disintegration of the old effeminate world:
> Authority, type-creating energy, self-elimination, discipline, protection of racial character, recognition of the eternal polarity of the sexes. . . . The idea of honor—national honor—does not permit Christian love, nor the humanity of the Freemasons, nor Roman philosophy.[49]

In other words, there is a special "ethical" mission inherent in and known intuitively by true Germans, and much of it concerns removing the virulent threat to the putative bioracial superiority posed by the existence of world Jewry. And there was no greater antisemite than Alfred Rosenberg (who was eventually convicted and hanged at Nuremberg).

In a word, it is not that the Nazis considered themselves "beyond good and evil" (to use Nietzsche's phrase), but rather they sought to define morality in terms of their own exclusivist concept of themselves. Secondly, it is how their self-selected morality or values would impact all other institutional practices that gave Nazism its immoral cast from the perspective of universal moral values and the intrinsic worth and dignity of all human persons. In this sense, I believe Fuller's view is closest to my own. However, it makes sense to raise the issue whether the Nazi "ethic" is truly a moral point of view or simply a moral pretense for brute domination (a view I think is closer to the truth), an idea at least as old as the discredited argument of Thrasymachus, immortalized by Plato in the *Republic*. It holds that "might makes right," or that justice (or goodness, rightness) is whatever is in the interest of the stronger (or presumably superior) party.[50]

AN OVERVIEW OF LAW UNDER NAZI RULE: TWO PERSPECTIVES

I return to a question raised earlier about a possible misconstrual of law under Nazism based strictly on American (i.e., non-German) legal and moral standards—the notion that 'only Germans can fairly judge Germans.' In my opinion, although it is true that certain important differences exist(ed) between pre-Hitlerite Nazi Germany and America (e.g., the principle of the binding value of precedents or stare decisis, the nature of "jury" trials, and so forth), these cannot excuse the kinds of irrational discriminatory, racist, and unfair laws; courts; judicial proceedings; interpretations and findings; and ultimate Nazi "values" that the German legal system only too readily embraced. Furthermore, it was the Nazi government itself, along with the still unbelievable sympathy and support it continued to receive from the German people generally, that spearheaded the effective nazification of the legal order. By placing itself (and its proponents) above "the law," its leaders and functionaries would not be held legally accountable by its own institutions for its atrocities. In mobilizing the German people for the purpose of fulfilling the aims of Nazism, Nazi totalitarianism forged a society that was determined to reject the rational, universalistic, and human values that some from German history itself had made the centerpiece of the European Enlightenment (e.g., as in Kantian ethical philosophy). In their place, arbitrary vicious discriminations based on race, religion, ethnicity, national origin, and sexual preference were given legal standing, the end result often being individual murders, organized extermination of an unwanted or "undesirable" people, and the overall corruption of civilization's stabilizing institutions. In this regard, the undeniable complicity of the German legal profession in furthering Nazism stands as a monument to the institutional subversion that an intolerant militaristic rights-denying, irrational society made possible. Moreover, there are no accessible rational and empirical grounds that would qualify those of so-called Germanic 'stock,' 'character,' or 'mind-set' to be the sole authoritative interpreters of German history, institutions, policies, and behaviors. Indeed, Kant's ethical philosophy, the centerpiece of the European Enlightenment, stands as an enduring internal monument against such insidious thinking.

The supreme 'rule of law' morally upholds the American democratic liberal tradition by mandating that citizens will be ideally (or reasonably) secure in the possession and enjoyment of their basic rights and will be protected from civil and criminal wrongs committed against them or their society. In principle, it mandates that the wrongdoer will be legally brought to account and compelled to make satisfaction in one or another way as prescribed by law either to the victim or to the public whose community is harmed by the prohibited behavior. In the protection of these basic rights generally, it also mandates that certain procedures must be observed in order to prevent unjust infringements on the possessor's substantive rights in the administration or enforcement of the law. Granted, there are many different sorts of rights, principles, and values that engage a system of law in a variety of ways. But, as Fuller explains, it is much too simplistic to conclude, then, that law remains law as in the case of Nazi law, regardless of its link to immorality, injustice, indecency, or evil.

Politics and Law in the United States

In the spirit of the idea of my preferred concept of the 'rule of law,' the prosecution process in the United States of America has historically reflected political influence on the legal and moral traditions associated with the Constitution. For instance, in what some have termed a "moral reawakening,"[51] an increased political demand has occurred in the late 1970s and 1980s for American society to deal officially with suspected Nazi war criminals who are living among us but whose rights of citizenship are well protected by our legal system.

This political demand brought about a fusion of politics, morality, and law, perhaps explained by the relaxation of the ties between the U.S. government's cold war intelligence interests and the anti-Communist beliefs of Nazi war criminals, about which I will have more to say in subsequent chapters. This demand created sufficient pressure in Congress to organize the Office of Special Investigations (OSI) as the investigative prosecutorial arm of the U.S. Department of Justice. Moreover, in this political climate, the lack of any legal provisions relating to 'war crimes' in the Criminal Code was noted. The political climate encouraged the use of the civil process in cases involving suspected 'war crimes,' even though the allegations concerned crimes committed on foreign soil by foreign nationals who have since become naturalized citizens of the United States.

In this case, a civil statute regarding denaturalization in effect but rarely enforced for many years has functioned as a basis to deprive a suspected war criminal of citizenship for the infraction of lying on his or her original naturalization application.[52] This application of the civil law clearly illustrates the primary political purpose behind such prosecutions. By denaturalizing suspected Nazi war criminals and expelling them after a legal process that concludes with a finding of 'guilt,' the law can place them by means of either deportation or extradition within the reach of a country whose laws and jurisdiction do provide a criminal process for dealing with them straightforwardly as war criminals. Why the U.S. Congress has not passed federal laws for the right to prosecute Nazi war criminals, at least those living in our midst, deserves an explanation that will be presented in the next Chapter 5. Unfortunately, too, from my viewpoint, an unfulfilled legacy of the Nuremberg trials is that still no authoritative international institution exists before which such criminal cases may be brought, viz., an international criminal court.

Politics and Law in Nazi Germany

In view of the ideal of the 'rule of law,' an objection may be anticipated that the administration of "justice" by the Nazis (e.g., the infamous People's Courts) also was motivated by political (though certainly not universal moral) considerations in influencing the legal process. So we may ask: Why is the American approach to ridding the United States of Nazi war criminals any less objectionable than that of the Nazis, who used their judicial system to rid their nation of designated "undesirables"?

The context for the most obvious response to this question lies ultimately in the set of key differences between an individual rights-based, constitutional democracy and a racist totalitarian dictatorship with respect to how a system of law is construed to function in each. For this context, we may turn to some of the writings of a noted German legal theorist, Carl Schmitt (referred to earlier in this chapter), whose prominence and presence in the Prussian State Council (which was under the de facto leadership of the influential Nazi Hermann Göring) and eventually his Nazi party membership contributed greatly to the Nazis' effort to legitimize its subversion of the rule of law.

SOVEREIGNTY AND THE "EMERGENCY DECREE": SUBVERTING THE RULE OF LAW

C. Schmitt held that a correct view of sovereignty must recognize "who decides in a situation of conflict what constitutes the public interest or the interest of the state, public safety and order." The "situation of conflict" is an exception, danger, or emergency (to the state, its authority) and as such is never codified in an existing system of law.[53] It is the true sovereign power that decides whether an emergency or a normal situation exists. Since law is always "political" and "situational," he believed, "the sovereign produces and guarantees the situation in its totality. He has the monopoly over this last decision." The correct juristic definition of sovereignty is not "the monopoly to coerce or to rule, but . . . the monopoly to decide." In addition, "authority proves that to produce law it need not be based on law,"[54] and "the Decisionist implements the good law of the correctly recognized political situation by means of a personal decision."[55] The sovereign "decides whether there is an extreme emergency as well as what must be done to eliminate it"[56] in the interest of stability and security.

Accordingly, he supported a controversial interpretation of the emergency provision of the Weimar Constitution (Article 48): "For the purpose of reestablishing public security and order the Reichspräsident may undertake measures and may suspend certain basic rights."[57] Finally, his totalitarian theory of law, rooted as it is in the consummate political and legal duty each has to the sovereign leader and to the German *Volk*, underscored the critical value of legally suppressing politically undesirable individuals and parties. He states:

> The endeavor of a normal state consists above all in assuring total peace within the state. . . . To create tranquility, security, and order and thereby establish the normal situation is the prerequisite for legal norms to be valid. Every norm presupposes a normal situation, and no norm can be valid in an entirely abnormal situation. As long as a state is a political entity, this requirement for internal peace compels it in critical situations to decide also on the domestic enemy.[58]

This is his "friend or foe" doctrine noted earlier. In 1932, the year before the Nazis came to power, he argued that extremists should be banned from political participation and that an "equal chance" should be given solely to those who clearly support the sovereign's exercise of power to preserve the German order.[59] Of course, the "legal" suspension of basic rights, the illegality of competing political parties, and the commitment to "law and order" above all considerations of "justice" are—and became—a prescription for repression, tyranny, and the practice of law in the Nazi Third Reich. C. Schmitt was the self-appointed Nazi theorist of law and politics, believing as he did that "he who possesses power makes laws"[60] (*potestas facit legem*). Even though sympathetic to the German legislature (the Reichstag) until it relinquished its lawmaking role to the Führer through passage of the enabling act,[61] which in effect superseded the Weimar Constitution and permitted Hitler to rule by decree, "Schmitt sanctioned the new reality in which political decisions emanated from the movement as embodied in the Führer, who was, simultaneously, the head of state."[62] This form of executive action declares what the law is and applies it, even prior to a decree. This process is very different from and antithetical to the "rule of law" as described in the following section with respect to the prosecution process.

THE RULE OF LAW CONTRA NAZI LAW: ON PROSECUTION

By examining our criminal 'prosecution process' more closely, we may further illumine why political choices are filtered and legitimized by the independent process of the 'rule of law' in the case of suspected Nazi war criminals, and also we may explain and defend why some overriding obligation exists to prosecute them under a civil, if not criminal, statute.

The meaning of the 'prosecution process' in our American constitutional liberal democracy involves 'substantive' and 'procedural' aspects of law, and these aspects apply to both civil and criminal matters. However, to illustrate the essentials of the 'prosecution process,' we may turn to the constitutional grounds for prosecuting a criminal case.

The 'prosecution process' receives its basic meaning, power, and priority from the Fourth Amendment to the Constitution, which states that "no Warrants shall issue, but on probable cause." The guiding substantive principle behind this procedural provision is that all citizens are presumed to possess an inviolable legal (and moral) right 'to be secure in their persons' and property against 'unreasonable searches and seizures.' This is a legal restraint imposed on government in its relationship with citizens and is the main thrust of the principle; however, the standard of reasonableness that governs the relationship is and has been subject to changing judicial interpretation—e.g., it is respectful of circumstance or good faith action by police—and is sufficient even without objective evidence. Further procedural support for restraint is found in the 'due process' clauses of the Fifth and Fourteenth Amendments: Neither government nor other agents may deprive a citizen of life, liberty, or property without 'due process' of law. Therefore, a search or seizure is allowable only for cause and never on the basis of suspicion alone.

Suspicion is not a crime (nor is a citizen 'under suspicion' a criminal). But when suspicion is supported by sufficient evidence of facts as defined by law and gathered as a result of an authorized investigation, suspicion gives way to 'probable cause' that someone has committed a crime.

The 'prosecution process' begins with an arrest warrant being issued for probable cause.[63] The burden of proof at this initial stage in a criminal proceeding "is to establish a reasonable ground for belief in guilt."[64] The presumption of the defendant's innocence carries through until the last stage where the defendant's *actual* guilt must be demonstrated "beyond a reasonable doubt." The 'prosecution process' ends with either a finding of guilt or of exculpation. Subsequent to a conviction, the question of penalty for wrongdoing arises, but this matter will be left untreated for now.

Although the 'prosecution process' as it is applied to Nazi war criminals in the United States seems at first glance to be consistent with our view of the supreme importance of the 'rule of law,' despite the absence of criminal statutes regarding 'war crimes,' it may be challenged: Is there an unequivocal prima facie obligation to prosecute suspected Nazi war criminals on civil grounds or any combination of grounds? As I intend to show, I believe the answer is affirmative.

The 'prosecution process' may go forward only if there are existing legal grounds on which to base a trial. For instance, in the British Parliament, the House of Lords tried unsuccessfully to prevent passage of 'war crimes' legislation that would allow prosecution of alleged Nazi war criminals in Britain. Interestingly, it was Sir Hartley Shawcross, chief British prosecutor at the Nuremberg trials, who expressed the prevailing sentiment in the House of Lords when he claimed that such a bill would be ex post facto law. Also, he believed that there is the related set of questions about the reliability of evidence from witness identification and the presumed futility of witness identification after forty-five years.[65] The House of Commons obviously disagreed and had the bill passed in May 1991 over the Lords' dissent. Perhaps they felt that the Nazi crimes were so horrendous that no suspected Nazi war criminal should be allowed to find refuge in the laws of Great Britain, no matter how much time has elapsed. And perhaps among their reasons for passing the bill (and defeating the ex post facto charge) was the argument that there is sufficient existing international and common law on which British domestic law may yield or be made to conform, i.e., to preserve a "higher law."

Moreover, the majority of the House of Commons must have recognized that despite the "frailties" of witness identification, not all witness-identification testimony is unreliable; and when combined with other types of compelling evidence such as alibi, written documentation, circumstances, and so on, the case can be—and has been—made to satisfy the most rigorous standards of criminal justice.

PHILOSOPHIZING ABOUT
PROSECUTING NAZI WAR CRIMINALS

An inquiry into arguments about the prosecution of Nazi war criminals is pertinent to philosophy not only because some prominent philosophers have acknowledged that it is but also because of the opportunity it offers for us to look afresh at the basic values that underlie our civilization. This is especially true in the context of a political democracy for, from the democratic perspective, a philosophical scrutiny promotes the standards and values of public debate about matters of public interest and facilitates information flow. Enlightened decisions may then be expressive of a concept of persons as rational, autonomous individual beings whose life plans are conceived and carried through within a system of basic rights meant to protect and promote the "existential" health of their possessors. An inquiry into arguments about the prosecution of Nazi war criminals is fully within the broader philosophical tradition: On the one hand, it may offer us a consistent and comprehensive account of what public policy is and should be and why or when it invites public support and acceptance. Further, it may elucidate which standards are relevant and defensible, weighing all significant factors. On the other hand, philosophy can analyze and inquire into practical aspects of public policy and itself be enriched by such involvement but without conceding too much to current realities. Indeed, this is what we now call "applied" philosophy. It is from this perspective that I connect the ethical values associated with democracy to the issue of prosecuting suspected Nazi war criminals.

In this vein, I would argue that the topic of what to do with the fugitive Nazi war criminal is not to be submerged entirely under the broader rubric of criminality, where it would be seen as merely one type of egregious crime to be understood in the usual course of criminal prosecutions. Certainly it has a cognate conceptual relationship to criminality in general, but it is also distinctively unique, not unlike political terrorism.[66] For instance, when certain acts of terror are labeled as "criminal," the acts become redefined with a relativity of ideology: X's terrorist is Y's 'freedom fighter.' But perspectival relativity is not an issue in the case of the Holocaust and its perpetrators, because to agree with or excuse them is nothing less than to undermine the values of a democratic, rights-based civilization in favor of the nihilist "values" of a society based on institutionalized racism, terrorism, and other unjust 'legal' policies and practices. Terrorists regard their victims as unavoidably expendable for a putative "higher" purpose; but the Reich regarded the victims of the Holocaust as *the "higher" purpose* itself; the goal was to rid the Reich (and eventually, the world) of all Jews.

AN OBLIGATION TO PROSECUTE IN A RIGHTS-BASED SOCIETY

Philosophers refer to a variety of obligations: moral, political, and legal. I will not argue here for a special understanding about how each type of obligation may be related to any other, for there is no shortage of theoretical possibilities in the history of philosophy. However, I shall argue that an 'obligation to prosecute' has as its central source and justification the ideal of a rights-respecting, 'constitutional' community.

Once we accept the view that it is among the government's most crucial tasks to protect, preserve, and enforce not only rights but also the obligations citizens have in relation to their community and to one another, government also becomes bound to protect and preserve the integrity of the constitutional system that mandates its authority. We should observe that this argument is directed to the level of what a system does about respecting *a body* of rights and not to the level of enumerating the specific rights that the system is geared to respect. Accordingly, a prosecutor's presumed obligation to prosecute is to be understood at the former level and is distinct from what legal constraints and compulsions may exist to prosecute at the lower level of enforceable rules or rights.[67]

The relationship between what is entailed in respecting a body of basic rights and what practices, principles, and policies are necessary for a system to respect specific rights is not mainly at issue unless the way a system unevenly respects, or fails to respect, or recognizes rights raises questions about the legitimacy and integrity of the system itself. It is a part of my claim that the rights of citizens are best secured by an obligation of government to preserve its own integrity, particularly in cases involving serious wrongdoings, by placing on trial the suspected wrongdoers to determine guilt. Failure to prosecute when sufficient evidence is available to support a belief in guilt signifies at once the system's apparent willingness to tolerate serious criminality. Although it may be true that prosecutorial discretion often places the prosecutor beyond the reach of judicial accountability, i.e., a prosecutor may elect not to begin a criminal prosecution, there are various jurisdiction-specific remedies available for a prosecutor's inaction, including a prosecutor's removal or criminal prosecution. Nevertheless, the basic principle that is assumed to guide the prosecutor is that a basic obligation exists "to enforce all criminal laws regardless of his own judgment of public convenience or safety," and that a failure to prosecute is prima facie in need of justification.[68]

Just as citizens have basic obligations to respect the basic rights of others in virtue of their own possession of similar rights, so it is claimed that a government within a system of basic rights has a basic obligation to secure that (constitutional) system that gives it its structural and operational mandate.

A most important abrogation of this governmental obligation may be found in its ultimate failure to distinguish between those who commit serious wrongs and those who do not, since basic to our own American community is a system of principles and rules that places limits on socially tolerable behavior and prohibits that which is not. Political, legal, or other social institutions give specific definition and enforcement to the system. Consequently, a failure to prosecute suspected Nazi war criminals is to tolerate suspected serious criminals alongside those for whom no such suspicion has been raised. Furthermore, it is to treat such suspects as if no evidence has been brought accusing them of committing the sorts of prohibited activities against which a community's system of rights must necessarily protect its members.

There is a vast number of suspected criminals who are not brought to justice, and this fact raises questions about the effectiveness, determination, and integrity of a legal system. But it also reflects discretionary problems associated with the prosecutor's role. The prosecutor is the port of entry into the judicial (criminal) process, but the process itself is not entirely precise, as suggested in reference to sometimes uncontrolled prosecutorial discretion.

LEGAL JUSTICE AND THE RULE OF LAW

In effect, the integrity of a system of rights invariably hinges on whether and how it administers legal justice in fulfillment of its obligation to do so. It is to be considered less valuable on what basis such suspects are prosecuted in order to determine guilt (i.e., civil or criminal) than on taking the necessary and appropriate steps to remove from our society those whose continued presence undermines the community's integrity. But often it takes the moral and political will to use (or enact) the appropriate laws and to establish jurisdiction and to overcome expected opposition to such prosecutions.

The thrust of my claim is that once a successful general defense is made for an 'obligation to prosecute,' a failure to prosecute is an important wrong done to the community as a whole (if not to individual members and victims alone). It would count as an exception when an equally important, competing claim not to prosecute exists in special cases, but then a special justification will be needed to establish their exceptional character while preserving the integrity of the system as a whole. The arguments I give in Chapter 7 against prosecuting suspected Nazi war criminals are attempts to provide this special justification, since none who make these arguments, to my knowledge, ever reject the general principle that criminals ought to be tried and, if found guilty, punished.

Before we address the cluster of arguments about prosecuting Nazi war criminals now and in the future, the constraints of time and old age being noted, some account must be given about the dispersion of Nazi war criminals following the defeat of the Reich, about some of the schemes involved in their resettlement, and about the problems confronted by those who tracked them down, gathered evidence against them that would stand up in court, and apprehended or had them arrested and placed on trial in domestic courts (since no international criminal court has been established).

NOTES

1. This section is a greatly modified and expanded rewrite of parts of an article of mine entitled "On the Issue of Prosecuting Nazi War Criminals" in Yehuda Bauer et al., eds., *Remembering for the Future*, vol. 2 (Oxford: Pergamon Press, 1989), pp. 1284–95. From *Trials of War Criminals Before the Nuremberg Military Tribunals Under Control Council Law No. 10*, vol. 3, (Washington, D.C.: U.S. Government Printing Office, 1951), pp. 984–85.

2. Burns Weston, Richard Falk, and Anthony D'Amato, *International Law and World Order* (St. Paul: West, 1980), p. 189; also, Louis Henkin, *The Rights of Man Today* (Boulder: Westview Press, 1978), p. 32.

3. For a well-documented account of the ways in which the Nazis destroyed Germany's legal justice system, see Ingo Müller, *Hitler's Justice: The Courts of the Third Reich*, trans. Deborah L. Schneider (Cambridge: Harvard University Press, 1991).

4. For a detailed account of denazification in U.S.-occupied Germany, see James F. Tent, *Mission on the Rhine* (Chicago: University of Chicago Press, 1982).

5. Surya P. Sinha, *What is Law?* (New York: Paragon House, 1989), passim. Sinha describes a number of different ideas regarding "the rule of law" as understood in theory and practice in various nations.

6. Thomas Buergenthal and Harold G. Maier, *Public International Law* (St. Paul: West, 1990), p. 9.

7. Article 2(7) of the United Nations Charter, quoted in Louis Henkin, *The Age of Rights* (New York: Columbia University Press, 1990), pp. 51–52.

8. "Constitution, Anyone? A New Cottage Industry, *New York Times*, February 2, 1990, p. B11; also "Rutgers Professor Flies the Globe Assisting in Constitution Writing," *National Law Journal*, December 11, 1989.

9. See Joseph W. Bendersky, *Carl Schmitt* (Princeton: Princeton University Press, 1983), pp. 227–29.

10. Müller, *Hitler's Justice*, pp. 10–11, 22, 24.

11. Ibid., pp. 16, 81.

12. Ibid., p. 23.

13. Ibid., pp. 23–24.

14. Ibid., p. 29.

15. David W. Zisenwine, ed., *Anti-Semitism in Europe* (New York: Behrman House, 1976), pp. 31–34.

16. Müller, *Hitler's Justice*, pp. 29, 60, 72, 74, 97.

17. Claudia Koonz, *Mothers in the Fatherland* (New York: St. Martin's Press, 1987), p. 192.

18. Ibid.

19. Whitney R. Harris, *Tyranny on Trial* (Dallas: Southern Methodist University Press, 1970), pp. 221–24.

20. Müller, *Hitler's Justice*, p. 39.

21. Ibid., p. 69.

.22. Ibid., p. 154.

23. Ibid., p. 148.

24. Peter Hoffmann, *German Resistance to Hitler* (Cambridge: Harvard University Press, 1988), pp. 109–10.

25. William L. Shirer, *The Rise and Fall of the Third Reich* (New York: Simon and Schuster, 1960), p. 1023.

26. Ibid., p. 1077–78.

27. Ibid., p. 269.

28. Hoffman, *German Resistance to Hitler*, p. 125.

29. John A. Appleman, *Military Tribunals and International Crimes* (Westport: Greenwood Press, 1971), p. 158.

30. Ibid., p. 158–62.

31. Müller, *Hitler's Justice*, p. 238.

32. Ibid., p. 74.

33. Ibid., p. 73.

34. Ibid., pp. 41, 129–30.

35. Ibid., p. 70.

36. A main element in this influential nineteenth- and early twentieth-century philosophy of law in Germany was the repudiation of universal moral principles associated with natural law theories in favor of state authority and its internal legal norms. See Bendersky, *Carl Schmitt*, pp. 9–10.

37. H.L.A. Hart, "Positivism and the Separation of Law and Morals," in R. M. Dworkin, ed., *The Philosophy of Law* (Oxford: Oxford University Press, 1979), pp. 17–37.

38. Lon L. Fuller, "Positivism and Fidelity to Law: A Reply to Professor Hart," in J. Feinberg and H. Gross, eds., *Philosophy of Law*, 3d ed. (Belmont: Wadsworth, 1986), pp. 98–102.

39. Ibid., p. 98.

40. Hart, "Positivism," p. 31.

41. Kenneth I. Winston, *The Principles of Social Order: Selected Essays of Lon Fuller* (Durham: Duke University Press, 1981), pp. 159–67.

42. From Lon Fuller's *The Morality of Law* (1964) quoted in John Arthur and William H. Shaw, eds., *Readings in Philosophy of Law* (Englewood Cliffs: Prentice-Hall, 1984), pp. 54–55.

43. Müller, *Hitler's Justice,* p. 296.

44. Ibid., p. 10.

45. Aural Kolnai, *The War Against the West* (New York: Viking Press, 1938), p. 279.

46. Quoted in H. J. Paton, *The Moral Law* (London: Hutchinson, 1981), p. 29.

47. Robert E. Conot, *Justice at Nuremberg* (New York: Harper and Row, 1983), p. 216.

48. Peter Viereck, *Meta-Politics: The Roots of the Nazi Mind* (New York: Capricorn Books, 1961), pp. 232–35.

49. Conot, *Justice at Nuremberg,* p. 216.

50. *The Republic of Plato,* trans. F. M. Cornford (New York: Oxford University Press, 1964), p. 18.

51. James W. Moeller, "United States Treatment of Alleged Nazi War Criminals: International Law, Immigration Law and the Need for International Cooperation," *Virginia Journal of International Law,* vol. 25, no. 4 (1985), p. 797.

52. See Sec. 340(a), 66 Stat. 260, 8 U.S.C.A. Sec. 1451(a). Also, see the ruling of the U.S. Supreme Court in Fedorenko v. United States, 449 U.S. 490, 101 S.Ct. 737, 66 L. Ed. 2d 686 (1981).

53. Carl Schmitt, *Political Theology* (Cambridge: MIT Press, 1985), p. 6; 'legal decisionism' is the label used to describe Schmitt's jurisprudence.

54. Ibid., p. 13.

55. Ibid., p. 3.

56. Ibid., p. 7.

57. Ibid., p. xxi.

58. Ibid., p. xxi.

59. Ibid., p. xxiii.

60. George Schwab, "Carl Schmitt: Political Opportunist?" *Intellect,* February 1975, pp. 335–36.

61. Conot, *Justice at Nuremberg,* pp. 120–21.

62. Schwab, "Carl Schmitt," p. 336; also see Kolnai, *War Against the West,* pp. 301–03; and Shirer, *The Third Reich,* p. 196.

63. J. Shane Creamer, *The Law of Arrest, Search and Seizure,* 3d ed. (New York: Holt, Rinehart and Winston, 1980), pp. 8–13.

64. Ibid., p. 13.

65. "Britain Moves to Allow Nazi War Crime Trials," *New York Times,* May 2, 1991, p. A7.

66. Although not all violence can be classified as an act of terrorism, the premeditated indiscriminate murder of civilians for certain political purposes carried out with a calculated "indifference to existing legal and moral codes" is. See Burton Leiser, *Liberty, Justice and Morals* (New York: Macmillan, 1986), pp. 393–413. A variety of responses to terrorism are discussed in Benjamin Netanyahu, *Terrorism* (New York: Farrar, Straus and Giroux, 1986).

67. The distinction between "being obliged" and "being obligated" is also found in H.L.A. Hart's, *The Concept of Law* (London: Oxford University Press, 1961), pp. 84–86. Hart was criticizing the early positivism of John Austin, who asserted that law is merely the command of a sovereign backed by a threat.

68. M. R. Kadish and S. H. Kadish, *Discretion to Disobey* (Stanford: Stanford University Press, 1973), pp. 80–85.

5

NAZI FUGITIVES:
THE ESCAPE FROM ACCOUNTABILITY

In Nazi Germany and Austria and in the formerly occupied territories of Eastern Europe, hundreds of thousands of Nazi war criminals, collaborators, Nazi sympathizers, and persecutors began preparations for postwar life and for their escape from accountability as the twelve-year span of the so-called Thousand-Year German Reich was nearing utter defeat. Indeed, well before the fighting stopped, the German business and industry elite held a secret meeting in Strasbourg in 1944 in order to map out a strategy to protect their financial interests and at least the spirit of the Third Reich, which they had so willingly embraced and supported from its inception.[1] Among those firms represented at the clandestine conference were I. G. Farben, the Thyssen steel works, the coal companies of Emil Kirdoff, the Krupp industries, and the Cologne banking interests.[2] Eventually the directors of some of these companies would be implicated at Nuremberg in the commission of crimes against humanity. However, by 1951, not one of the disappointingly few convicted officers was still incarcerated, and most managed to escape prosecution altogether.[3]

THE DISPERSION OF NAZI WAR CRIMINALS

At the war's end, millions of people throughout Europe whom the war either uprooted or who volunteered to work in Germany began to return to their homes. However, informed sources indicate that there were at least 1 million displaced persons (DPs) unwilling or unable to return to the homes they had known before the war.[4]

Under the auspices of the Allies, assembly centers or camps for displaced people were hurriedly set up. Almost immediately the administrative personnel were inundated by pressures for care and resettlement. Compounding these problems is the fact that these were gathering locations for the innocent victims of the war and of the Nazi terror as well as for the many tens of thousands of murderers and persecutors whose motives for relocation differed dramatically from those of other displaced persons. The motives of the latter group centered on an escape from accountability; and many of these DPs eventually became the infamous "quiet neighbors" in the United States, of which a chief prosecutor for the Justice Department's Office of Special Investigations spoke in the early 1980s.

Of course, it is also true that hundreds of thousands of people who actively contributed to war crimes also remained at or returned home, blending into the ordinariness of everyday postwar life and seeking to conceal their nefarious wartime activities, both to the Allies and to the surviving victims. They sought to avoid prosecution and retaliatory vengeance, and many sought as well to reinstate themselves to their former jobs or posts of influence, power, and authority. Often they were successful, thereby further subverting Allied efforts at denazification. Elaborate conspiracies of silence, cover-up, disinformation dissemination, and the suppression of culpatory evidence were characteristic of most postwar European communities that shared complicity in Nazi atrocities. However, not all antisemites went underground. Even after the war ended, the spillover of Jew-hatred into the postwar period is exemplified by the Kielce pogrom that resulted in murders of forty-one Jews and the beatings of at least seventy-five more. "The Poles in Kielce—men, women, and children—beat Jews mercilessly, squeezed their genitals, crushed bones, broke legs, tore off limbs and mutilated bodies in the most barbaric fashion." Often the police and local militia assisted violent expressions of hostility toward Jews while officials of the Roman Catholic church maintained a nonintervention posture.[5]

Generally, underground railroads were put in place in order to camouflage the true identities of the more prominent war criminals, to forge travel documents, to transfer plundered wealth out of Germany, and to open escape routes to countries that were willing to give them sanctuary for self-interested political or economic reasons. Too often the persecutors and murderers were, on the surface, indistinguishable from others who were seeking a safe haven from the wreckage of war, provided that they were among the preferred "national" groups from the prospective host country's point of view. Besides, many of these immigrants with a Nazi past simply concealed their criminal involvements by lying on their immigration papers.

THE U.S. INVITATION TO NAZI WAR CRIMINALS

A government's unevenhandedness in immigration policies with respect to the European DPs is one thing. However, the deliberate searching out and bringing of former Nazis to America is quite another. In this vein, a significant number of cases have been widely publicized concerning an intentional scheme by some U.S. officials to locate former Nazi scientists and technologists/technicians, falsify their identities, and bring them to the United States. In spite of their criminal activities during the Nazi period, the upshot of this scheme by a coterie of government and military officials was the enlistment of Nazi expertise in the burgeoning anti-Communist struggle against the Soviet Union. Naturally, the Nazis who benefited from this scheme were placed, at least for a time, beyond the reach of the forces of prosecution, including U.S., British, and French.

THE RELOCATION AND REINTEGRATION OF NAZIS AND NAZI COLLABORATORS

Confronted by the imminent prospect of being prosecuted by the IMT or by domestic courts in a number of countries, some Nazi leaders committed suicide (e.g., Hitler, Martin Bormann,[6] Heinrich Himmler, and after his capture, Joseph Goebbels) rather than face a trial, and others killed themselves prior to execution (viz., Hermann Göring) or else were executed (Hans Frank, Alfred Rosenberg, and Gestapo chief Ernst Kaltenbrunner); some were tried on lesser offenses; and others were acquitted. Nevertheless, many major war criminals remained at large even though some were eventually caught and tried and, in some cases, executed (e.g., Eichmann). But too often the persecutors received nominal sentences on conviction for serious crimes including murder, and insufficient or suppressed evidence forestalled or derailed prosecutions of many others. In short, only a minority of planners and perpetrators were ever brought to trial, though these cases number in the thousands. For there were hundreds of thousands of Nazi activists who took advantage of having a Nazi government and of wartime conditions to persecute, enslave, murder, and enrich themselves by plundering the wealth of millions of innocent victims. Some of this wealth, in combination with counterfeit money, was surreptiously used to secure a variety of escape routes and to pay off those who assisted in the dispersion process and also to fund many Nazi expatriots as well as the governments of their host countries. It was also used to covertly reestablish social institutions and professional personnel with Nazi backgrounds, particularly in postwar Germany—from politicians, professional university personnel, judges, and business and industry leaders to local civil servants and police officials.

My chief concern is to argue the case for sustained efforts at subjecting the remaining unprosecuted Nazi war criminals to a fair judicial process. The sweep of my claim is intended to include not only those who have never before been placed on trial for Nazi crimes but also those who were not properly prosecuted for lesser crimes when in fact justiciable evidence indicates the commission of more serious crimes.

THE EVASION OF JUSTICE

There are a number of reasons for how and why so many Nazi war criminals have remained fugitives from justice. To illustrate some of the most important of these reasons, I have selected the cases of certain individual Nazi fugitives that amplify the way in which whole groups of such people managed to evade prosecution or to help others escape the judicial process. Again, my focus lies primarily on the "unprosecuted" or the "improperly prosecuted" and less on those who received nominal or unjustly shortened penalties—though these matters are of related concern—since it may be argued that any judicial process is better than none in establishing even a skeletal public record of minimal legal accountability and of serving the interest of justice.

PUVOGEL AND FRÄNKEL: REINTEGRATION

The Nazi judicial system and the German legal profession have already been briefly discussed in Chapter 4. The cases of Hans Puvogel and Wolfgang I. Fränkel remain significant in this regard because they demonstrate how about 50 percent of the members of the legal profession after the war had a hand in refocusing official attention away from prosecutions of Nazi offenders. As the beneficiaries of this process of diversion, most of these people managed either to escape prosecution themselves or to conceal evidence of their own Nazi backgrounds or those of others. In what helped to shape a climate of forgetfulness, many judges and prosecutors from the Third Reich found reemployment in the West German legal system.[7] Hence, as one might expect, there was not much sympathy in the judicial system for removing tainted officials. For example, "Dr. Hans Puvogel, author of a dissertation containing the pleas for the 'removal of inferior beings through killing,' was named minister of justice in the state of Lower Saxony in 1976." It is reported that "when a judge drew public attention to the dissertation, disciplinary proceedings were opened not against Puvogel but against the judge! He was officially reprimanded, for by publishing the information he was guilty of failing to show the proper respect to his superior."[8]

Another typical case concerned W. I. Fränkel, who was a department head at the Reich Office of Public Prosecutions during the Nazi period:

> [He] was responsible for a large number of pleas of nullity, entered against "overly lenient decisions": the president of the Stuttgart Court of Appeals,

Richard Schmid, once referred to him as a "fanatic on the death penalty."
On March 21, 1962, Fränkel was appointed prosecutor general of the
Federal Republic. An investigation into his past was closed by the Karlsruhe
Court of Appeals on September 3, 1964, with the remarkable argument that
no evidence existed to prove that Fränkel, by now the highest-ranking
prosecutor in the country, has ever "even doubted the validity of the regulations named . . . during the war, let alone recognized their invalidity."
After Fränkel's past, which he had artfully concealed, became known to the
public, it still took months to force his resignation, and he has continued to
receive a full pension to this day.[9]

Again, these two cases attest to the failure of the denazification of
Germany's professions. Much has already been published about the
complicity of the German medical establishment in not opposing the
illegal and immoral experiments on concentration camp inmates and
about the continued influence and good standing of the Nazi "health
care" providers and the students trained by them.[10]

ADOLF EICHMANN:
THE MONASTERY ROUTE AND
THE SOUTH AMERICAN CONNECTION

The case of Adolf Eichmann, the desk-based director of the "Final
Solution," illustrates how many members of the Nazi brass were given
refuge and brought to sanctuary in South America (e.g., in Argentina,
Paraguay, Bolivia, Chile, and Brazil) with the help of a German Vatican
insider, Bishop Alois Hudal (the rector of Instituto Santa Maria dell'
Anima), of other charitable Catholic societies ("which suddenly remembered . . . humanitarian duties"[11]), and covert organizations like Odessa,
the Organization of the Ex-Members of the SS, formed in 1946. Although
the church has been credited with saving almost 50 percent of Rome's
Jews by hiding them in places like monasteries, religious orders such as
the Franciscans (Roman Catholic priests) actually provided refuge for
escaping Nazis. They assisted Odessa by forging the so-called monastery
route between Germany/Austria and Italy. This route was the most
important of a number of alternate routes criminal Nazi fugitives, like
Eichmann, were channeled through by Odessa and its church-related
abettors of criminals, "from one monastery to the next, until they were
received in Rome," and by a Franciscan monastery that became a transit
camp for Nazi criminals[12] until the Vatican could arrange visas for them
to South America.[13] After leaving Prague in 1945 and hiding in U.S.
internment camps, Eichmann himself was "channelled to Rome by a
Croat committee, using the 'monastery route,' and had arrived there in

the late summer of 1950. The committee was headed by followers of the head of the Croat collaborationist government, Ante Pavelic." With Odessa's support, he evidently obtained a Vatican passport to Argentina.[14] "In Perón's Argentina the Nazis were well-received and exercised considerable power; they were the organizers of the Argentinean army, experts in Argentinean industrialization, and their money added to the liquidity of Argentinean banks. Eichmann could feel secure in Argentina."[15] Eventually, Simon Wiesenthal, the Austria-based pursuer of Nazi criminals, helped to establish Eichmann's whereabouts in Buenos Aires (Eichmann was now calling himself Ricardo Klement). The Israeli secret service (the Mossad) then seized him in Argentina in May 1960 and brought him to Israel to stand trial for ordering, under Himmler's command, the round-up and deportation of Europe's Jews to the death camps. According to Eichmann's report to Himmler in August 1944, almost 4 million Jews had been murdered in "various extermination camps while an additional two million met death in other ways, the major part of which were shot by operational squads of the Security Police during the campaign against Russia."[16] Eichmann was tried, convicted, and executed in Jerusalem in 1962.

Two important questions continually arise in connection with both the manner in which Israeli agents seized—or as some put it, kidnapped—Eichmann in breach of the sovereignty of Argentina, and the legitimacy of Israel's assertion of jurisdiction in Eichmann's case since the State of Israel was not in existence at the time the defendant's crimes were committed. Indeed, most nations have refused extradition requests by Israel on the latter basis, whereas critics who espouse the former argument typically claim that the illegal kidnapping and breach of state sovereignty nullify any indictment against Eichmann. These questions will be better addressed in Chapter 6, where I discuss the nature of culpability and responsibility for Nazi war crimes and as well the obligation for bringing Nazi war criminals to justice.

JOHN DEMJANJUK:
THE U.S. DISPLACED PERSONS ACT OF 1948

The case of John Demjanjuk (who was convicted in 1988 by an Israeli court for being the Nazi "Ivan the Terrible") will be cited to illustrate how Nazi war criminals, particularly collaborators, were enabled to evade prosecution in such large numbers because the United States, but also Great Britain and Canada, welcomed them as displaced persons. As of 1992, Demjanjuk has appealed his conviction and death sentence for the crimes he was charged with committing at the Treblinka death camp in Poland. The charges against him were crimes against the Jewish people, 'crimes against humanity,' 'war crimes,' and 'crimes against persecuted people'[17] pursuant to the appropriate provisions of Israel's Nazi and Nazi Collaborators Law (enacted in 1950). In addition, Demjanjuk has been advised that the Italian Justice Ministry is still considering murder charges against him for crimes allegedly committed while he served at a concentration camp in Trieste.[18] Two other developments in the Demjanjuk case must also be noted. First, as of August 1992, the U.S. Court of Appeals for the Sixth Circuit in Cincinnati, Ohio, is reconsidering its 1986 decision honoring Israel's extradition request because Demjanjuk's lawyers are claiming that the OSI prosecution team suppressed alleged exculpatory evidence. Second, the Israeli Supreme Court has been given newly acquired documents released from former Soviet files that allegedly bear on the issue of whether Demjanjuk was "Ivan the Terrible" of Treblinka and whether as an SS guard he may have committed war crimes at Sobibor, another notorious Nazi death camp.

Along with the many thousands of Nazi criminals and collaborators (especially those from Eastern Europe) who sought to meld with the hundreds of thousands of displaced persons at the war's end, John Demjanjuk entered a DP camp, or assembly center, in Germany under the joint control of the Allied military forces and the United Nations. The Allied military command has been described as "having herded Jewish concentration camp survivors . . . together with non-Jewish DPs, many of whom had been their former guards and tormentors, or with Nazi collaborators. . . ."[19] In an egregiously insensitive application of a policy of nondiscrimination, the Allies were seen as treating surviving Jewish DPs as the Nazis did—except that the Jewish DPs were not being murdered.[20] The process of burying the past for most Nazis was about to begin in earnest.

Whereas the Soviet Communists had for the most part coercively repatriated the refugees under their control, U.S. policy was different. The United States soon became a new home for most DPs who opted not to return home and live under communism. It was the Displaced Persons Act of 1948 passed by the U.S. Congress that opened the floodgates to the United States for waves of predominantly Eastern European immigrants. It seemed that the provisions of the act were designed to exclude the foremost victims of Nazism, the Jews, while most likely including the persecutors along with the other DPs who sought a home elsewhere. The UN International Refugee Organization (IRO) had set as a condition for a formal request for a visa to a country other than one's own country of origin that the petitioner had to establish DP status before being placed in a pool for those seeking a country willing to open its doors for immigration. Another condition required the screening of the applicant by the officials of the country to which one sought a visa. It was by this route that Demjanjuk and so many other alleged Nazi war criminals found refuge: They were "invited" to come to the United States.

Following the war, Demjanjuk lived in two DP camps (Landshut and Regensburg), became a licensed truck driver, took a wife, and eventually passed beyond the poorly supervised and scrutinized procedures that were prerequisite to procuring a visa, thereby meriting permission to exit the DP camps. He has said that his first choice was Argentina and Canada his second, because he was determined not to be repatriated to the Ukraine, his native country, under Communist rule. Finally, after being employed as a truck driver for the U.S. Army, Demjanjuk applied for a U.S. visa in 1951. In 1952, he, his wife, and a new daughter arrived in the United States as immigrants and settled in a suburb of Cleveland, Ohio, where he acquired employment as an engine mechanic at the Ford Motor Company. In 1977, Demjanjuk was charged by the State of Israel with being the infamous Ivan the Terrible of the Treblinka death camp.[21] In the United States, on the assumption that he lied on his citizenship application, steps toward his denaturalization commenced. The United States has no war crimes statutes under which to try suspected war criminals. Therefore, Demjanjuk was given a civil trial. The ultimate purpose of the civil proceedings was to revoke his citizenship and deport him, either to his native Ukraine or to some other country willing to place him on trial for war crimes. In my opinion, in spite of the track record of a large number of Nazi war criminals who managed to live as quiet neighbors, no civilized society ought to permit murderers to live quietly in its midst. Demjanjuk was denaturalized and stripped of his U.S. citizenship by a Federal District Court in Cleveland, Ohio, in 1981 for lying (and also incriminating himself) on his citizenship application. In 1986, after his appeals were denied, Demjanjuk was extradited to Israel to stand trial for war crimes. In 1988 he was convicted by an Israeli court and was given a death sentence. As of 1992, his sentence is on appeal to Israel's Supreme Court.

The shape taken by the discriminatory DP Act of 1948 was influenced by a complex mix of antisemitism, anti-Communism, and strong anti-alien sentiments as well as by a certain ironic spirit of generosity toward certain groups. It was adjudged to have been "written to exclude as many concentration camp survivors as possible and to include as many Baltic and Ukrainian and ethnic German Volksdeutsche [ethnic Germans] as it could get away with."[22] The plain meaning of the U.S. Displaced Persons Act was to permit 200,000 DPs to enter over a two-year period.[23] A *New York Times* reporter observed that "it is easier for a former Nazi to enter the United States than for one of the Nazis' innocent victims,"[24] because it was nigh impossible to identify individuals with a Nazi background given the inadequate training and small number of screening agents, the mass of DPs awaiting processing, the widespread bias for Eastern Europeans who were non-Jewish, and the rampant falsification of DP documents (as well as deliberate falsehoods on subsequently filed immigration and naturalization papers). "By the time the Displaced Persons Act finally expired on June 30, 1952, nearly 400,000 immigrants had come to the United States under it. Some 337,000 (85%) of those were DPs, the rest were Volksdeutsche."[25] An informed estimate is that almost 10,000 Nazi war criminals were virtually welcomed to a new life in the United States.[26] It is obvious, then as now, that the exclusion of Nazi war criminals was not of sufficient importance to the policymakers.[27] Consequently, such infamous war criminals were permitted entry to America under the 1948 Displaced Persons Act as Andrija Artukovic, Karlis Detlavs, Albert Deutscher, Feodor Fedorenko, Liudas Kairys, Juozas Kungys, Karl Linnas, and Valerian Trifa.[28]

ARTHUR RUDOLPH: THE U.S. INVITATION TO GERMANY'S SCIENTISTS

Although these DPs with Nazi backgrounds were able to slip through the screening process quite easily, there were a number of Nazis and passionate supporters of Nazis given deliberately covert passage to the shores of the United States. Some of Germany's finest scientists were pressed into service in the escalating cold war with the Soviet Communists, what with the latter's attempt to capture technology and material from former Nazi lands now under their control. (The Communist revolution in China did not occur until 1949). By 1948, almost 500 scientists had applied for visas to the United States, backed by relatively secret but official sponsorship.[29] In this connection, the name Arthur Rudolph comes to mind, for he was a production manager and engineer at the Nordhausen concentration camp, a close associate of rocket scientist SS Major Werner von Braun (both were from the Peenemünde, Germany, group), and a committed Nazi SA member.[30]

In the course of their work on behalf of the German war effort, von Braun and Rudolph are reported to have accepted slave labor brigades totaling some 60,000 individuals appropriated from the Buchenwald concentration camp. It was unusual for these forced laborers to survive more than six months. For this reason, they have been described as being "less than slaves." A prosecutor from the Nuremberg trials, Benjamin Ferencz, explains his coinage of this apt phrase: "The Jewish concentration camp workers were less than slaves. Slavemasters care for their human property and try to preserve it; it was the Nazi plan and intention that the Jews be used up and then burned."[31] The goal was to produce rockets. The method used minimized labor costs to the Reich, while simultaneously exploiting concentration camp inmates and down the line productively contributing to "the Final Solution." Upward of 25,000 people apparently died, mainly from excavating underground tunnels under conditions of light, air, food, and medical deprivations. "On average, one hundred men a day died of exhaustion, starvation, and disease, or were murdered by the SS guards, either on a whim or as punishment. . . . Replacements supplied by the SS from other concentration camps arrived on demand from Rudolph."[32] Surely Rudolph did not create these inhumane conditions, but neither did he hesitate to utilize slave labor in advancing the manufacture of rockets.

At the center of the conspiracy to bring Nazi scientists and technicians to the United States were the Joint Chiefs of Staff who devised a plan to achieve this goal.[33] Soon 350 German scientists came to the United States, along with 100 rocket experts, in execution of the Pentagon's Operation Paperclip. Secrecy was crucial, but it became a "managed secrecy," that is, to dilute any likely public outrage that German Nazis were being imported if the facts became known. So the Joint Chiefs issued a "sensitively handled" press release on October 9, 1945, which asserted that certain criteria had been used for German scientists admitted to America. For instance, each must be shown to be "indispensable to the successful accomplishment of the most vital military research program," "carefully selected," and "brought on a voluntary basis" for a "temporary stay." The press statement patently affirmed that "certain outstanding German scientists and technicians are being brought to this country to ensure that we take full advantage of those significant developments that are deemed vital to our national security."[34] Worries about public outrage, admission of war criminals, or sabotage from within America were also brushed aside in favor of the arms race.

The U.S. Office of Special Investigations of the Justice Department cites an interrogator's memo regarding Arthur Rudolph: "100% Nazi, dangerous type, security threat."[35] Admission to the United States of Rudolph and others like him with a criminal Nazi past was a convincing demonstration of the operative principle of realpolitik that complicity in war crimes is secondary in importance to scientific and technical expertise. (There is no question that abundant evidence of the use of forced labor was available to the Joint Chiefs since Nuremberg prosecutors even made it publicly accessible during the trials; although the forced labor camps were SS created and supervised, the targeted scientists clearly were implicated.) Rudolph and about 117 rocket-team experts were relocated by 1947 to a desert area in Texas to assemble some V2 rocket parts shipped from Germany.[36] Although Rudolph had gained the attention of U.S. war crimes investigators, coupled with eyewitness testimony against him at the Dora-Nordhausen war crimes trial, questions put to the Nazi scientists, including Rudolph, were met with a conspiracy of silence, pleas of ignorance, and evasions.[37]

Evidence of Rudolph's subterfuge regarding his degree of responsibility for war crimes began to surface, but the most implicating admissions were expurgated by the Pentagon from his and many others' security files.[38] In 1982, Arthur Rudolph, by then a U.S. citizen with a distinguished career as a director of America's successful Saturn V rocket project in the Apollo program (responsible for America's first moon landing) was interrogated several times by the OSI about his Nazi past (about his role in the use of slave labor at Nordhausen and the Mittelwerk underground rocket factory, and the doctoring of his U.S. security report). In these interviews, he acknowledged some responsibility for "demanding extra labor to build rockets . . . while being aware of the conditions under which such work was performed." The OSI informed Rudolph that it would press a legal challenge to his citizenship. Faced with this prospect, he chose to renounce his citizenship and return to Germany with a large U.S. pension and NASA honors for his leadership role in the U.S. space program rather than endure a denaturalization hearing. This turn of events enraged the so-called Paperclip Germans, who believed that America should be grateful for the scientific and technical services they provided. In Rudolph's words: "I helped put the first man—an American—on the moon and then I was treated like this. . . . The Americans are very ungrateful and I am very bitter."[39] This complaint was uttered by Rudolph in Hamburg, Germany, in 1986. According to more recent information, he was in Canada (and then returned once again to Germany) awaiting authorization from Washington to return to the United States to clear his name, claiming, among other things, that he was coerced in 1984 into an agreement to leave and that West German authorities had since found "no evidence to justify war crimes charges"[40] against him in spite of his admissions of guilt and ardent support for the Nazi mission. However, Canadian immigration officials held a deportation hearing against him in absentia, where it was claimed that new evidence has emerged showing that Rudolph was in fact a mastermind of the Nazi scheme to force inmates of concentration camps to become "less than slaves." In view of this development, there is also an effort under way in the United States to strip him of the prestigious Distinguished Service Medal awarded to him by NASA officials.

KLAUS BARBIE:
THE U.S. CONTRIBUTION TO THE "RAT LINE"

Another well-known Nazi war criminal is Klaus Barbie, a Gestapo head in Lyons, France, during the war. He was convicted of crimes against humanity by a French court in 1987 and sentenced to life in prison (France had abolished the death penalty). Some members of the U.S. Counter Intelligence Corps (CIC) recruited him after the war for intelligence work. In return for his CIC work, the U.S. State Department and High Commissioner's Office assisted Barbie in resettlement in Bolivia. In 1942, Barbie had been installed to assist in the command of Gestapo activities in Lyons, among which were the torture and murder of Jean Moulin, a leader in the French Resistance, and the deportation of forty-four Jewish children from a village called Izieu (near Lyons) to the Auschwitz death camp. As the war ended, Barbie was apprehended in Germany by U.S. forces. The Counter Intelligence Corps induced Barbie to work for it as an agent from 1947 to 1951. Evidently the only agency handling Barbie during this period was the CIC. French overtures toward placing him on trial for war crimes spurred his escape to Italy under the protection of the CIC. His value as a CIC agent assured Barbie of the necessary assistance in reaching Italy and concealing his identity under the alias Klaus Altmann. Barbie received approval to go from Italy—the landing cite for many fugitive Nazi higher-ups—to South America. Throughout his pre-Bolivian immigration, the CIC protected their "agent," the "Butcher of Lyons," as he was efficiently moved in 1951 through the so-called rat line. However, some key documents about how the CIC decisions involving Barbie were made are reportedly missing from his file, according to Allan Ryan, Jr., a former OSI director.[41]

Nevertheless, the broad outline of official U.S. help, done for the CIC's own reasons in helping Barbie to escape accountability, is indisputable. What is not known, however, is whether in the recruitment of Barbie CIC officials knowingly and deliberately gave illegal cover and protection to a war criminal (who was sought by the French, an ally of the United States). The conclusion drawn from the investigations conducted many years later by the OSI was that although Barbie was known as a Gestapo official, it was not clear from any evidence at the time of the CIC's handling of Barbie that he was a war criminal. The French government wanted him to be prosecuted, so suspicions were evidently in the air. But by June 1950, his war crimes record was established and that "not to cooperate with efforts to obtain Barbie's surrender, and by its [CIC personnel's] false statements to HICOG [the United States High Command for Germany] on June 16, 1950, that Barbie's whereabouts were unknown, responsible officials of the Army interfered with the lawful and proper administration of justice," i.e., they deliberately obstructed HICOG from discharging "its lawful obligation to effect the extradition of war criminals."[42] In winning the U.S. government's apology to the French government in the Barbie affair, the OSI report (of Ryan's) concludes: "By snatching Barbie from the French judicial process and spiriting him half-way around the world," CIC officials "had violated the fabric of justice under law that holds together all democratic societies." The United States acknowledged in 1983 "the wound it had inflicted on the commitment to the rule of law, a commitment that America shares with all civilized nations."[43]

In 1983, Barbie was expelled from Bolivia, his home for more than thirty years, by a civilian government that transported him to French Guyana where he was seized by French officials and flown to France to stand trial. In Barbie's own words in denial of the charges against him, "I fought a harsh combat against the Resistance, which I respect, but it was war, and now the war is over."[44] With these words, Barbie—and innumerable other war criminals just like him—dismissed the crimes against humanity that they committed under the pretext of war. Barbie was found guilty on all 341 accounts of the indictment, including illegal deportation and imprisonment, torture and murder. He was convicted in 1987 on charges of crimes against humanity and sentenced to life in prison, where he died in 1991.

JOSEPH SCHWAMMBERGER:
GERMAN BUSINESS ASSISTANCE IN
THE RELOCATION OF FORMER NAZIS

It has been estimated that over 7,000 former Nazi officers found a haven from the reach of prosecutors in Europe in Argentina alone (again, this was true of Eichmann also). The case of Joseph Schwammberger is a good illustration of the help a Nazi fugitive received from both an underground network and a German company (with a Nazi past) in an escape from justice and in resettlement (and employment) in another country.[45]

Seventy-nine-year-old Schwammberger was placed on trial in June 1991 in the reunited Germany after having been extradited from Argentina, where he had been living since 1949, to Germany in May 1990. He was accused of murdering at least 3,377 people—many by his own hand—mostly Jews in Nazi-occupied Poland.[46] A court in Stuttgart convicted him of committing hundreds of murders, including that of a rabbi who refused to work on the holiest day of the Jewish year, Yom Kippur. The now eighty-year-old Schwammberger received a life imprisonment sentence on May 18, 1992. The former Nazi SS lieutenant was the commandant of two forced labor camps (Przemysl and Mielec) in which almost 100 surviving witnesses described how, for his own sadistic entertainment, he unleashed dogs to tear bodies of inmates, used pliers to wrench prisoners' gold teeth from their mouths, personally smashed the heads of children against a wall, shot many other people at point-blank range, and threw men, women, and children into bonfires, according to the Simon Wiesenthal Documentation Center, which gathered evidence against Schwammberger to be used at trial.

Wiesenthal reports (in Vienna, January 31, 1988) that Schwammberger resided in a town near Buenos Aires, Argentina, and worked for a subsidiary of a German firm, Siemens, a company implicated in war crimes, e.g., for using slave labor and for building death camp barracks; however, for lack of sufficient evidence in 1945–1946, its directors were not prosecuted.[47] Evidently, Schwammberger had entered Argentina in 1949 with an Italian passport, but according to Wiesenthal, the Italian government denied that it had issued a passport to him. In efforts to locate Schwammberger, Wiesenthal reports, Siemens was asked to disclose where his pension payments were being sent. Siemens refused to provide the information.

In 1945, Schwammberger was arrested in Austria by the police. He was caught with a cache of plundered jewelry, watches, and gold teeth, obviously extracted from his victims. (The government of Austria auctioned the valuables as "unclaimed property," says Wiesenthal). He was placed in a French internment camp, Oradour, in Austria. He escaped from Oradour in January 1948 with the assistance of Odessa,[48] the Nazi underground organization, according to claims by the Vienna-based Jewish Documentation Center.

ALOIS BRUNNER:
THE MIDDLE EAST CONNECTION

The last case of a Nazi fugitive I will mention is that of the infamous Alois Brunner, who is believed to be living in Damascus, Syria, under the protection of Syrian President Hafez al-Assad. It is a destination that Brunner had in common with Franz Stangl (at least until he moved to Brazil), the commandant of Treblinka, who, according to Wiesenthal, was responsible for 700,000 murdered Jews.[49] (As an aside, Stangl was routed through Rome in his escape, where the Catholics were assisted by Bishop Hudal, who obtained a Red Cross passport for Stangl; Protestants found temporary asylum with Praeses Heinemann). In Wiesenthal's words, Brunner implemented "the general staff plan for the extermination of the Jews" that Adolf Eichmann drew up. "Eichmann demanded that the Jews should be registered, assembled and deported—Brunner registered, assembled and deported them."[50] Wiesenthal's estimation is that

Brunner's claim to fame was the introduction of the idea of Jewish collaboration. In the end, Brunner's main regret, expressed in interviews, is that he was "unable to complete cleansing the world of Jews."[51] To earn his status as a war criminal, he had deported 14,000 Jews from Slovakia to Auschwitz and Treblinka,[52] 47,000 Viennese Jews, and 50,000 Greek Jews from Salonica, which "cleansed" the ghetto entirely (a fact "known to the entire German occupation force in Greece, with the exception of Kurt Waldheim").[53]

As the war ended, Brunner made his way back to West Germany after being expelled from Czechoslovakia. He used the name Alois Schmaldienst and earned a living as a truck driver for the U.S. Army occupying Germany. Brunner received an Egyptian visa under the name Georg Fischer and left for Cairo. As Wiesenthal attests, the Germans were much in demand by Middle East countries as experts on a variety of matters. The Syrians eventually admitted Brunner in 1954, once his true identity was revealed to them, for Syria had a high regard for Brunner's role in the murder of Jews. Moreover, Brunner would feel safe from deportation or extradition because it was not likely that Syria would expel him for killing Jews.[54] France, Germany, and Austria have all requested extradition, but as of 1992, Brunner continues to live in a villa guarded by Syrian police.[55] Evidence suggests that warnings were sent to Brunner about investigations by German prosecutors into his Nazi war crimes. These warnings were reportedly conveyed by the German Red Cross, an organization whose officials after the war are known to have "helped vast numbers of Nazi criminals flee overseas, by arranging forged papers for them in cozy cooperation with Bishop Hudal."[56] On June 29, 1991, Germany and France moved jointly to have Syrian authorities extradite Brunner.[57] Perhaps Syria may be willing to include Brunner's expulsion as part of an initiative for promoting Middle East peace talks with Israel.

SUMMARY

From the information presented in this chapter, it should be sufficiently clear that the majority of Nazi war criminals and their collaborators have evaded prosecution. Many of these fugitives are still alive, living out the twilight of their lives in the security of years of identity concealment and assimilation into their respective communities of sanctuary, often with the protection of the host governments. Their escape from legal accountability was the result not only of individual craftiness and subterfuge and of the assistance provided by the collapsing Nazi Reich but also of a series of support systems from well-financed underground organizations, antisemitic legislative prerogatives and policies, and the perceived political necessities of host countries. German industrialists and leading Nazi officials transferred immense amounts of ill-gotten wealth abroad so as to enable escaping Nazis to establish "businesses, become partners in major enterprises, and, if necessary, bribe the authorities."[58] To be sure, many Nazi war criminals remained behind to wait out or undermine the postwar waves of denazification, to regain their posts and jobs, and to help other persecutors to bury their pasts and evade prosecution.

Apart from the reborn efforts in many countries to find and prosecute these Nazi fugitives (about which I will say more in Chapter 6), it seems that an unexpected but small-scale nemesis of some surviving Nazis is their own children or grandchildren who, like the young German girl in the recent film *The Nasty Girl*, discovered what horrible, unconscionable things her father (and in some cases, mother) did during the war. However, one can only wonder with dismay why many more young Germans, Austrians, and others from Eastern Europe do not raise questions publicly about their parents' generation and the Nazi Holocaust instead of insisting on not being burdened with the sins of their countrys' past, to let the past go. In my opinion, both the surviving murderers of the past and those of the future must be assured that civilized society condemns not only the evasions of justice but also the toleration of and assistance given to the Nazi fugitives.

NOTES

1. Benjamin B. Ferencz, *Less Than Slaves* (Cambridge: Harvard University Press, 1979), pp. 28, 34, 70.
2. Simon Wiesenthal, *Justice Not Vengeance* (New York: Grove Weidenfeld, 1989), p. 50.
3. Ferencz, *Less Than Slaves*, p. 32.
4. Allan A. Ryan, Jr., *Quiet Neighbors* (New York: Harcourt Brace Jovanovich Publishers, 1984), p. 8; Leonard Dinnerstein, *America and the Survivors of the Holocaust* (New York: Columbia University Press, 1982), pp. 9–22.
5. Dinnerstein, *Survivors of the Holocaust*, pp. 107–8.
6. Wiesenthal, *Justice Not Vengeance*, p. 105.
7. Ingo Müller, *Hitler's Justice: The Courts of the Third Reich*, trans. Deborah L. Schneider (Cambridge: Harvard University Press, 1991), pp. 208–18; see especially p. 214.
8. Ibid., pp. 213–14.
9. Ibid., pp. 215–16.
10. For instance, see Wiesenthal, *Justice Not Vengeance*, p. 118ff; and E. Ben Gershom, "From Haeckel to Hackethal: Lessons from Nazi Medicine for Students and Practitioners of Medicine," *Holocaust and Genocide Studies*, vol. 5, no. 1 (1990), pp. 73–87; Alan S. Rosenbaum, "The Use of Nazi Medical Experimentation Data: Memorial or Betrayal?" *International Journal of Applied Philosophy*, Fall 1989;

Robert J. Lifton, *The Nazi Doctors* (New York: Basic Books, 1986); Harmut M. Hanauske-Abel, "Politics and Medicine," *Lancet*, August 2, 1986, pp. 271–73.

11. Wiesenthal, *Justice Not Vengeance*, p. 54.

12. Ibid., p. 55.

13. Ibid., p. 61.

14. Ibid., pp. 70, 74.

15. Ibid., p. 76.

16. Whitney R. Harris, *Tyranny on Trial*, (Dallas: Southern Methodist University Press, 1989), p. 313.

17. Tom Teicholz, *The Trial of Ivan the Terrible* (New York: St. Martin's Press, 1990), p. 296.

18. *Response* (publication of the Simon Wiesenthal Center at Los Angeles, California), vol. 9, no. 3 (August 1988), p. 3.

19. Dinnerstein, *Survivors of the Holocaust*, p. 13.

20. Ibid., p. 43.

21. Teicholz, *Trial of Ivan the Terrible*, pp. 41–49, 338.

22. These people were the "'German ethnics of the East'—the notorious Nazi Fifth Column" (Ryan, *Quiet Neighbors*, p. 17).

23. Ibid., pp. 16–17.

24. *New York Times*, August 30, 1948; quoted in Ryan, *Quiet Neighbors*, p. 17.

25. Ryan, *Quiet Neighbors*, p. 25. His information came from *The DP Story: The Final Report of the United States Displaced Persons Commission* (Washington, D.C.: U.S. Government Printing Office, 1952), table 2, p. 349. A breakdown of the DP statistics may be found in Dinnerstein, *Survivors of the Holocaust*, pp. 273–90.

26. Ryan, *Quiet Neighbors*, p. 26.

27. Ibid., p. 28.

28. Ibid., pp. 353–60. Andrija Artukovic (Croatian) was extradited from the United States in 1986 and convicted of war crimes in 1986 by Yugoslavia; he died in prison while an appeal of his death sentence was pending. Albert Deutscher committed suicide in 1981 immediately subsequent to the OSI's denaturalization action. Feodor Fedorenko (Ukrainian) was executed by the Soviets in 1987 for war crimes after he was deported from the United States in 1984. Luidas Kairys (Lithuanian) had his U.S. citizenship revoked in 1984. He was ordered deported in 1987. Juozas Kungys (Lithuanian) was an accused Nazi war criminal who agreed in 1988 to be stripped of his U.S. citizenship in return for pernament status as a resident alien. Karl Linnas (Estonian) was deported from the United States in 1984 to the USSR. He died in a Soviet prison in 1987 before the Soviets could decide whether to retry him or to affirm his death sentence (decided in 1962 in absentia). Valerian Trifa (Romanian) had his U.S. citizenship revoked in 1981. He was deported to Portugal in 1984. These are only some of the more than eighty-three cases filed through July 1, 1984, by the Immigration and Naturalization Service or the Justice Department's Office of Special Investigations. Some of the information on each individual noted was provided to me by John K. Russell, the OSI's special assistant to the director and investigator, Criminal Division of the U.S. Department of Justice.

29. Tom Bower, *The Paperclip Conspiracy* (Boston: Little, Brown, 1987), p. 242.

30. Ibid., pp. 111, 204.

31. Ferencz, *Less Than Slaves*, p. xvii.

32. Bower, *Paperclip Conspiracy*, p. 112.

33. Ibid., p. 125.

34. Ibid., pp. 131–32.

35. Ibid., p. 120.

36. Ibid., p. 200.

37. Ibid., p. 201.

38. Ibid., p. 240.

39. Ibid., p. 277.

40. *New York Times*, July 10, 1990.

41. Ryan, *Quiet Neighbors*, p. 306.

42. Ibid., p. 318.

43. Ibid., p. 321.

44. *New York Times*, July 4, 1987.

45. Most information on the Schwammberger case has been supplied by the Simon Wiesenthal Documentation Center, Los Angeles, Calif.; Research Director, Aaron Breitbart.

46. *Plain Dealer* (Cleveland), July 18, 1991.

47. Tom Bower, *The Pledge Betrayed* (Garden City: Doubleday, 1982), p. 331.

48. Wiesenthal, *Justice Not Vengeance*, p. 48.

49. Ibid., p. 85.

50. Ibid., p. 233.

51. Ibid., p. 234.

52. Ibid., p. 242.

53. Ibid., p. 239.

54. Ibid., p. 76.

55. Ibid., p. 243.

56. Ibid., p. 250.

57. *Plain Dealer*, June 29, 1991.

58. Wiesenthal, *Justice Not Vengeance*, pp. 49–50.

6

POST-NUREMBERG PROSECUTIONS AND THE PROBLEM OF BLAME

THE PERSISTENCE OF ANTISEMITIC INSENSITIVITY

Some prominent thinkers and activists assert that in view of the Nazi Holocaust we are no longer entitled to indulge the traditional belief in humanity's moral and religious sanctity. According to philosopher Robert Nozick, humanity has lost its status of intrinsic moral value.[1] Richard Rubenstein has construed the Holocaust to be the fulfillment of the nineteenth-century Nietzschean prophecy about the impending "death of God" because it shattered the credibility of any reference to transcendental standards of morality and (divine) justice.[2] Religion professors Alice L. Eckardt and A. Roy Eckardt have underscored Christian complicity in the Holocaust. They write that "from the day of Original Sin, the Holocaust became possible" because of "the church's persisting *adversus Judaeos* tradition." Furthermore, they argue that once the enormity of the Holocaust is fully acknowledged, a reconstructed Christian theology without its antisemitic core elements of triumphalism and supersessionism becomes a necessity because of the linkage between Christian belief and Jewish suffering (especially in the Holocaust).[3]

Frankly, it is impossible for me to believe that all human beings have, by virtue of their humanity or possession of reason, a core of genuine goodness that shines through from time to time in spite of the pervasive influence of passion and ignorance on behavior. Confronted with the retrospective spectacle of the deliberate and unspeakable suffering, pain, and murder of over 1 million innocent Jewish children at the hands of the Nazis and their millions of well-wishers, supporters, and assistants in persecution, I could not believe otherwise, particularly since the Germans as a people are not less nor more human than any other people. In fact, the rife persistence of virulent antisemitism and persecutions of the Jews in formerly nazified Europe and in most of the republics of the disintegrated Soviet Union speak volumes about why the vast majority of Nazi persecutors successfully managed to escape prosecution and live out their lives among family, friends, and host governments in relative obscurity, security, and peace. The subterfuge of "political necessity" has customarily been a major reason expressed by officials of governments for refusals to investigate and bring charges against Nazi war criminals, for cover-ups of identities and implicating information, reduction of sentences of convicted war criminals, or for pardons granted them outright. For instance, John J. McCloy, War Department official and postwar U.S. high commissioner in Germany, was responsible for unjustly pardoning or reducing the sentences of many Nazi war criminals. Indeed, he also was the person who advised President Roosevelt against bombing the railroad lines used for deportation to Nazi concentration camps, which, if successful, might have seriously slowed down the efficiency of the Nazis' extermination process.[4]

A much later instance of the outrageous subversion of justice toward convicted Nazi war criminals occurred by action of the newly independent government of Lithuania in September 1991. The Lithuanian government was reported to have issued thousands of certificates exonerating and rehabilitating Lithuanian Nazi war criminals convicted by Soviet courts. The certificates are said to proclaim that despite confessions by some to committing mass murder (primarily against innocent Jewish civilians), the recipients are innocent from the Lithuanian government's viewpoint.[5] Innocence by government proclamation instead of being established by judicial process, particularly when incriminating evidence is available against some of the worst persecutors, is at best a sacrifice of judicial integrity and justice for the expedience of appeasing popular anti-Soviet and nationalistic sentiments and perhaps latent antisemitism that discounts the value of Jewish lives.

In my opinion, this action is only an official manifestation of the prevailing antisemitism in Lithuania.[6] Jewish concerns and sensitivities are customarily discounted or ignored both in Lithuania and in many other parts of Europe, particularly in Nazi or Holocaust-related affairs. The Lithuanian government might have initially opted to retry these collaborators and persecutors in their own courts if they so distrusted the Soviet judicial findings. But that response was not of primary interest to them. Instead, the government prima facie pardoned convicted self-confessed mass murderers and other war criminals. Perhaps adverse public opinion and international pressure may yet persuade the Lithuanians to face their past squarely; but even if this reckoning were to come to pass, I expect that only very few of the worst offenders would be brought to justice; the rest would have little or no difficulty assimilating or being assimilated into the "new" (post-Soviet) Lithuania. Silence and inaction by the world community, which amount to tacit consent, will only fan the fires of antisemitism; Nazi persecutors will go unprosecuted and unpunished; future generations will point to few prosecutions and ask whether what the Nazis did was really so bad, which is precisely what the Holocaust-deniers seek; and future persecutors will be encouraged, reasoning that they too will get away with it.[7] Hence it is the world's tolerance of both overt and subtle forms of antisemitism and racism that may, under favorable conditions, beget another attempt at genocide against the Jewish people or against another persecuted group; it is this awareness that greatly distresses me. In this vein, it is law professor Alan Dershowitz's words that cut to the quick. He correctly observes that the ultimate desanctification of humanity was not only the Holocaust but also "humankind's *response* to that indescribably horrible event."[8] Sadly, the response is continuing, and the returns are not optimistic. It makes me wonder what the world has learned about community, moral goodness, and justice from the Holocaust. First and foremost, the world must acknowledge responsibility for prosecuting Nazi war criminals and all those who assisted in persecution. A "new world order," envisioned as rising from the ashes of communism and based on a strengthened capitalism, will lack basic moral integrity and justice unless accounts are properly and fully settled with remaining Nazi war criminals: Governments are obligated to prosecute them, as well as to educate their people about the Holocaust.

BRINGING NAZI WAR CRIMINALS TO JUSTICE IN DOMESTIC COURTS

In the years since the immediate postwar Nuremberg trials, thousands of Nazi war criminals have been brought to trial in the domestic courts of many countries. The postwar expectations that an international criminal code would be framed and an international criminal court established to prosecute the war criminals and the persecutors of the Third Reich, given the international character of Nazi crimes, have remained unrealized. Thus domestic legal systems and their courts have assumed legal responsibility for prosecuting primarily those Nazi and Nazi collaborators whose crimes of persecution were committed by "nationals" within their own jurisdictions. The extraordinary nature of Nazi crimes often required extraordinary domestic legislation enabling the court system of a given country to handle such prosecutions—which they usually have done with great reluctance, belatedly, and only after sufficient political pressure has been brought against the respective government. (The passage of appropriate legislation 1991 by the British Parliament to prosecute Nazi war criminals residing in Britain, after Parliament was wracked by internal dissension on the matter, is a case in point.[9])

SOME ISSUES SURROUNDING ISRAELI PROSECUTIONS

One country that enjoyed almost universal support among its citizenry for the speedy adoption of such legislation was Israel. Established as the "sovereign State of the Jewish People," Israel gained its independence in 1948 in the historical homeland of the Jews primarily as a response to the Holocaust, to the indifference and "closed doors" of most nations that confronted those Jews attempting to escape the Nazis' "Final Solution," to the antisemitic persecutions and pogroms that have plagued Jews for thousands of years, and ultimately to the need for permanent security for the Jewish people. Of course, many of Israel's citizens were native Jewish inhabitants who were joined by Jewish refugees from the slaughterhouse in Europe and by Jewish expatriots from Arab countries fleeing Arab persecution. Subsequently, Israel's Nazi and Nazi Collaborators Law was enacted in 1950.

Israel was one of a number of countries that incorporated many of the international legal notions articulated for the Nuremberg trials, particularly laws making genocide a crime; the criminalization of antisemitic, racial, and ethnic persecution; or laws based on 'crimes against humanity.'[10] In addition, a major impact of the Nazi Holocaust on international law was the Genocide Convention of the United Nations that became law on January 12, 1951; more than ninety countries ratified this international agreement, thereby binding the signatories to prosecute those individuals responsible for the crime of genocide, regardless of whether the perpetrators themselves committed genocide-related crimes or reside within or beyond the jurisdiction of the prosecuting nation.[11]

A succinct review of some of the problems encountered about or by Israel in prosecuting Nazi war criminals is instructive because legal and moral resolutions of these problems have been all but ignored by the uninformed Nazis' defenders and antisemites. Witness the resurrection of these arguments in the media during the Demjanjuk trial, more than twenty-six years after they were sufficiently addressed in the Eichmann proceedings in Israel.

Eichmann's Abduction and the Issue of Sovereignty

The first problem, which surfaced even before the Eichmann trial began, concerned the abduction of the accused by Israeli agents from Argentina in clear violation of its territorial sovereignty. (In international law, a nation's sovereignty over its internal affairs is in most instances virtually absolute.) Eichmann, we recall, had supervisory responsibility over the Gestapo's arrangements to murder hundreds of thousands of Jewish people and others disfavored by Nazis. Argentina lodged a protest with the United Nations over the incident. The problem was resolved when the disputants issued a joint communiqué in which both Israel and Argentina regarded the incident as "closed," Israel conceding that it "infringed fundamental rights of the state of Argentina."[12] Nevertheless, this concession was offset by a number of other considerations. Israel and Argentina did not have an extradition treaty and, even if they did, Argentina would likely have refused Israel's request to have Eichmann extradited to Israel since in the past the Argentine government would neither prosecute nor deport known Nazi war criminals residing in Argentina.[13] Moreover, no other country sought to exercise criminal jurisdiction over Eichmann. For instance, Eichmann's request to be extradited to the Federal Republic of Germany was denied by Germany. Further authority to justify the only option available to the Israelis is found in the international legal principle "extradite or prosecute," which means that safe haven anywhere must be denied to individuals who commit serious crimes—of the magnitude of Eichmann's—under international law.[14] As one legal expert writes: "In view of the moral imperative involved, a war crimes trial should be undertaken by the state most willing to do so," viz., Israel.[15] Finally, it has been established that Eichmann could not use the defense of forcible abduction, i.e., being brought to Israel involuntarily to stand trial, because Israel, like the United States, has a rule that the accused "may not oppose his trial by reason of the illegality of his arrest or the means whereby he was brought within the jurisdiction of that state."[16]

The 'Universality' Principle

Another problem that challenges Israel's legitimate right to apprehend and prosecute Nazi war criminals and whose resolution was well established in the Eichmann case centers on Israel's reliance on the 'universality' principle. To legally discharge their responsibility under international law, "the courts of all nations would be deemed to have jurisdiction over the offense" of genocide, war crimes, or crimes against humanity.[17] This is called the 'universality principle of jurisdiction.' It states that "some crimes are universally recognized as so opprobrious that any state that captures the perpetrator is entitled to try and punish the criminal on behalf of all nations of the world."[18] In the case of the extradition of John Demjanjuk to Israel, Nuremberg was cited to justify universal jurisdiction.[19] Legal precedence has established that individuals may be prosecuted in a suitable court of law anywhere for committing the crime of piracy because it is a serious offense against the law of nations. The Nuremberg trials were also justified on the 'universality' principle that crimes had been committed that were an unspeakable offense against "the common law of nations."[20] Israel based its jurisdiction on the "universal character of the crimes in question and their specific character as intended to exterminate the Jewish people." Israel roots its explanation in the "precedent of universal jurisdiction over piracy," the analogy of piracy to Nazi atrocities (despite obvious differences), and the application of the 'universality' principle in prior war crimes trials.[21] The "very special tragic link between the Nazi crimes" and "the establishment of the State [of Israel]," the fact that Israel is "the State of the Jews" and as well "the sovereign State of the Jewish people"[22] are also considerations that allow Israel to circumvent the anticipated charge that neither Eichmann nor Demjanjuk threatened Israel's security, nor were their victims Israelis.[23]

Ex Post Facto Denied: The Successor State Doctrine and the Crime of Murder

The last significant problem that Israel has had to face in its war crimes prosecutions—which is unique to Israel—concerns the fact that Israel acquired its political independence *after* the crimes in question were committed. Israel has discounted the importance of this problem[24] as it denied that it was applying its Nazi and Nazi Collaborators Law retroactively in violation of an ex post facto prohibition. Israel contended that it "was acting solely as an organ of the international community"—and to its benefit—because the horrible nature and extent of the accused's crimes shook the "international community to its very foundations," thus entitling Israel to invoke the principle of 'universal' jurisdiction.[25] But also Israel's law was merely giving "retroactive effect to statutes that reach back to acts subject to universal jurisdiction as a matter of customary law when committed, a substantial safeguard would be maintained against legislative abuse because the number of such crimes would also be limited."[26] In other words, the crime of murder—including mass murder and, even more so, genocide—is *malum in se* and is recognized as such by all civilized societies.

For instance, Chief Judge Frank Battisti (Eastern Division of the United States District Court of Northern Ohio), in his memorandum ordering Demjanjuk's extradition to Israel, reasons that Israel's "statute does not declare unlawful what had been lawful before; rather it provides a new forum in which to bring to trial persons for conduct previously recognized as criminal. . . . At the time in question, the murder of defenseless civilians during wartime was illegal under international law" (and this is supported in United States law).[27] The ex post facto prohibition denotes the creation of a new crime under which previous actions are subject to prosecution, and it is this action that offends the rule of law. Battisti correctly affirms that Israel's law is jurisdictional and not retroactive.[28]

Finally, Israeli courts have affirmed their legitimate entitlement to prosecute individuals accused of perpetrating war crimes before Israel's independence, arguing that they are courts of a 'successor state.' Israel has affirmed of itself the 'successor state' doctrine in the Eichmann case,[29] and Battisti cited it in the Demjanjuk case. "The criminal law defining and prohibiting murder in the State of Israel today incorporates the 1936 Criminal Code that was in effect in Palestine, pursuant to the authority of the United Kingdom, as Mandatory Power for Palestine under the League of Nations."[30] The 1936 Criminal Code prohibited murder, and Israel never moved to invalidate the code. Thus "Israel, as the successor state, can try persons for murders committed during the time of the British Mandate." Since Mandatory Power might have consistently passed "a law providing for the prosecution of extraterritorial war crimes . . . Israel's statute is not jurisdictionally defective because it was promulgated after Israel became a state."[31] Again, my review of the peculiar set of problems that Israel has encountered simply demonstrates that, in law and morality, Nazi war criminals ought to be prosecuted. It is, among other considerations, the responsibility of the community of nations, and of each nation, to see to it that this is done, now.

INTERNATIONAL RESPONSIBILITY FOR PROSECUTING NAZI WAR CRIMINALS

Other elements that have been cited that form the core of international responsibility to prosecute Nazi war criminals (besides fulfillment of obligations from international agreements) include: (1) respect for the rule of law; respect for the principles that murderers and persecutors of innocent, unarmed civilians must not be permitted to evade prosecution and that statutes of limitation for Nazi atrocities must be rescinded or else extended by the nations who have them (such as Germany); (2) respect for citizenship, for the moral value that acquiring and enjoying the protection of citizenship of a country under false pretenses is wrong, viz., concealing one's criminality, which if known would usually foreclose the option of citizenship.[32] In this regard, a statutory basis for denying a visa for entry into the United States to a person who assisted in the persecution of individuals (or groups) "because of race, religion or national origin" is found in the Refugee Relief Act of 1953.[33]

Given the resources, the national will, and suitable laws, the domestic prosecutors of countries that place Nazi war criminals on trial or deport them to other countries for trial must decide against whom they will bring charges and on what grounds the charges will be pressed. Some case history in the United States indicates a thicket of problems associated with any inquiry into the question of who is to be held responsible for Nazi atrocities, even if most of the Nazi leadership had survived and evaded prosecution. In general, I believe that all those who knowingly and willingly "assisted in persecution" in any of its forms or who failed to resist performing persecutory actions are certainly morally, if not legally, responsible. That said, attempts to characterize "assistance in persecution" encounter problems anyway.

ASSISTANCE IN PERSECUTION: WHO SHOULD BE PROSECUTED?

Chief among these problems is the matter of ultimately distinguishing between victimizer and victim. Clearly, victimizers persecuted or assisted in persecuting civilians; victims were those who suffered from acts and methods of persecution directed against them. The word "persecution" in this context generally means affliction or harassment so as to distress or injure—or even murder—someone for reasons of race, religion, or politics. These days we call such acts of persecution "hate" crimes.

One criterion has been suggested by some United States courts for determining assistance in persecution. It concerns whether a person has personally participated in persecutory acts or knowingly made more than minimal contributions to a group (including a "state") whose objective is (was) to persecute innocent civilians.[34] A difficulty that a legal expert notes about this criterion, as we shall see, is one that results in interpretive inconsistencies in judicial decisions. In the effort to conceptualize 'the victimizer,' the following issue must be resolved. Should an individual be held responsible for the persecutory consequences of a group's enterprise if the specific behavior or group role of the individual was itself nonpersecutory? Some cases have been mentioned that show that in the United States courts have not addressed this issue in a conceptually consistent manner.

One set of judicial interpretations of the "assistance in persecution" statute exemplify one side of the issue.[35] A court held in one case that the statute requires "proof of personal active assistance or participation in persecutorial acts."[36] Another court applied this interpretation when, to the disadvantage of the government prosecutor's case, the government could prove at best only that the defendant had "passively accommodated the Nazis, while performing ministerial tasks . . . which by themselves cannot be considered oppressive."[37]

Two cases have been cited that illustrate the other side of the issue, viz., that individual members may be blamed for assisting in persecution only if they knowingly performed nontrivial tasks (which in themselves were nonpersecutory) for an organization whose primary purpose was persecuting civilians. In one case, although the prosecution could not prove specifically that the defendant had personally committed acts of persecution, the court inferred from 'the evidence as a whole' that the defendant was aware of the persecutory mission of his organization and so is not blameless for the collective outcome (the U.S. Supreme Court refused to hear this case on appeal).[38]

In another court case, it was decided that a defendant had assisted in persecution when he admitted that he reported to police that certain civilians had sold food to Jewish civilians and that he had brought Jews not wearing the required ("Jewish identification") armbands to police.[39] In this case, it is not clear that the defendant was a member of a determinate group whose goal was to persecute innocent civilians nor is it evident that his specific actions were clearly nonpersecutory; however, the social context of the defendant's behavior (viz., the Holocaust) surely was a matter of organized and deliberate persecution. In general, these are cases where lower-level individuals are being held responsible for participation in persecutory outcomes of collective efforts; these cases may be seen as the counterpart to the 'command responsibility' doctrine that has been applied toward implicating an organization's authorities when as individuals their behavior was nonpersecutory in the sense that they gave orders to others to carry out persecutions but did not perform the acts themselves.

In many instances, the role of victimizer has been reasonably easy to establish. For example, in the cases of the Nazi and collaborationist governments, there were the heads of state who marshaled the resources of the state in planning, ordering, and carrying out the policy of genocide. The defense of 'sovereign immunity' is rejected as a shield to prosecution in such cases, as the Nuremberg precedent has established. Also, there were many criminal organizations whose 'collective' purpose was to execute the commands of their leaders and of the heads of state, e.g., to rid the land of the designated 'undesirables'—the Jews, Gypsies, and others—by ever-more-efficient mass murders. The mass slaughter at Babi Yar, a place on the outskirts of Kiev in the Ukraine typifies this example because it was at this location that over 35,000 Jewish people were brought by the SS Mobile Killing Units and massacred in thirty-six hours of constant shooting on September 29 and 30, 1941.[40] Others who could be classified clearly as victimizers were death camp guards whose job it was, among other things, to force their victims into gas chambers; to pull the switch; to humiliate, torture, or mutilate as the impulse struck; and to keep the gas engines running smoothly. Later some of these sadistic guards attempted to explain and excuse their brutality by claiming that the Nazis had coerced them into being camp guards and performing their assigned tasks under threat of death or repatriation to a hated Communist regime in control of their native countries. But since these guards were customarily sent to special SS training centers and eventually fulfilled their jobs of serious abuse and physical violence with a certain brutish enthusiasm and relish, a degree of voluntariness is attributable to them that undermines their "excuse" of coercion.

There were still other victimizers whose types and degrees of involvement in Nazi persecutions ranged from being routine engineers of railroad trains, whose human cargo was destined for the slave labor camps or crematoria, to rocket scientists and engineers who deliberately made use of slave labor to accomplish their production goals. There were also the professionals—from church officials and Nazi physicians to professors and lawyers, i.e., those who preached antisemitism and xenophobia and who glorified nationalism from the pulpit; those who engaged in cruel and inhuman experiments on unwilling, captive human test subjects; or those who used the classroom or their posts as educators to indoctrinate students in antisemitism, applaud the aims of Nazi totalitarianism, and/or expel Jewish educators or political opponents;[41] or those who designed unjust discriminatory statutes, prosecuted innocent people, or judged them guilty summarily and subjected them to disproportionately unfair and excessive penalties. And there were the industry and business moguls who financed the Nazi atrocities and who produced the technology to facilitate the killings. They built the death camps, manufactured the pesticide Zyklon B (used to kill the prisoners at Auschwitz), and used slave labor in the production process (e.g., five chief executive officers from I. G. Farben were convicted of "slavery and mass murder" at Nuremberg).[42] We should also include among the ranks of the persecutors those who benefited or expected to benefit economically from the Nazis' dispossession of the wealth of the victims of persecution. In fact, Franz Stangl, the commandant of Sobibor and Treblinka death camps, claimed that the primary "reason for the extermination of the Jews was that the Nazis were after their money."[43]

Victimizers and Victims

In each of the aforementioned cases the line of demarcation between victimizer and victim should now be evident. Accordingly, we may observe certain features that individual victimizers share qua victimizer. In its 'core' meaning in this context, a 'victimizer' is a person who knowingly and deliberately plans to cause or has caused, by word or deed, or who has economically benefited from the unwanted and unjust suffering of another person(s) for the presumed good of the victimizer, not of the victim. Of course, the paradigm of such victimization is the unjust, purposeful infliction of unwanted physical pain, injury, or death on a victim, though we must acknowledge that there are countless species of suffering, human-made or otherwise, that human beings have been made to endure. I focus only on the most objectively discernible type of suffering to illustrate my point.

Notice that all the key elements are present for making the victimizer responsible for the victim's suffering: intent, awareness, means, opportunity, and application. Therefore, individuals in the uppermost echelons of their organizations or individuals who were acting in their capacity as professionals are to be considered victimizers who committed 'justiciable' offenses (at least by Nuremberg standards) because they caused or assisted in some nonremote way in the persecution of innocent (mainly Jewish) civilians. They are also tangible contributors to the pervasive climate of religious, racial, and political oppression—what in retrospect became the cultural breeding ground for the exterminative outcome. In this case, the victimizers are subject to moral censure, if not legal blame, because of their deliberate repudiation or subversion of universal moral standards and principles of decency and human conscience. In other words, I think it is important to unmask the concealments that Nazi bureaucracy and technology seem to have provided the ordinary citizen in separating the person from his or her complicity and sense of responsibility for the evils wrought by the Nazis.

In addition, as Hannah Arendt has claimed, the routine nature of the evil done as a consequence of an individual's 'doing his job' in a large, reinforcing social system where every person is just 'doing his job' is banal because it masks from view the evil results of one's behavior and one's contribution to it.[44] Nevertheless, what helps unmask this inauthentic concealment by routinized behavior and bureaucracy is a recognition that "evil is the refusal to count the fates of others as if they counted as much as one's own fate counts to oneself."[45] In this sense, victimizers are evildoers and so are morally responsible and blamable for the evil that they do.

Conceptualizing Responsibility

As we now move toward conceptualizing the outer perimeters of responsibility, which involves an attempt to clarify the nature and extent of complicity of ordinary citizens in the Holocaust and Nazi war crimes, it has been essential to identify elements at the core of responsibility. Ultimately, the perimeters of responsibility must be established for resolving the lingering issues about the imputation of the "collective guilt" of the German people, not only during the Nazi period but afterward also, in view of current disreputable revisionist approaches to German history, a surge of neo-Nazi activity, widespread and familiar sentiment among Germans to prevent (Russian) Jews from (re)settling in

Germany, and the popular appeal of the 'apologetics' of the Nazi period by some adult children of prominent Nazis (such as the son of Rudolf Hess, deputy Führer of the Nazi party).[46]

Active and Passive Contributors to Persecution

Admittedly, there are a great many contributing factors to the Nazi Holocaust, and there are some relatively clear cases of complicity that are not invariably amenable to differentiation along victimizer/victim lines, because victimizers may be active or passive contributors in the process of victimization (the latter being more difficult to identify) and also because the type of participation in question generally is more remotely associated with specific acts of or assistance in persecution. The question is, of course, how remote is 'remote' to be considered too remote for the attribution of responsibility for wrongdoing. Later I shall describe obvious examples of cases that tend to discredit or invalidate any notion of collective criminal guilt. However, I am unwilling to dismiss completely the idea of collective *moral* guilt. This, too, I shall discuss.

Passive Victimizers

There are at least two senses of 'passive' contribution to wrongdoing that I intend, and both are meant to imply some degree of moral if not legal responsibility for the evils wrought by Nazism. A 'passive' contributor is not invariably the opposite of 'active' contributor in that the individual does nothing to affirm or encourage the wrongdoers or wrongdoing or refuses to or does not support the opposition; instead, a 'passive' contributor may be an activist whose actions or expressed attitudes promote, affirm, or clearly accommodate wrongdoing, the wrongdoers, and/or the climate of (Nazi) hatred, intolerance, and persecution. The other sense of 'passive' contributor is to permit the affiliation of oneself with a criminal organization and/or a group whose proclaimed purpose is the persecution or support for the persecution of innocent people, despite that one may "do nothing" or belong for "benign" reasons of social standing, privilege, opportunity, and so on. Holding membership in such Nazi organizations is a prima facie reason to believe in the moral and/or legal blameworthiness of each individual member proportionate to the role, behavioral consequences, and function of the organization in the Nazi system. Certainly, mere membership in a criminal organization is itself a criminal offense (the Einsatzgruppen were criminal organizations, the Nazi Women's Bureau—to my knowledge—was not).

Take the case of mothers and women generally in the Third Reich. Approximately 11 million German women (of a population of about 30 million) were mobilized to further the aims of Nazism on the home front.

What better place to ply the indoctrination process about the marvels of Nazi bioracial supremacy and its enemies (especially the Jewish people). Many women indoctrinated their families about the virtues of obedience to the fatherland, of antisemitism, and of a boycott of Jewish-owned shops. The women were organized under the leadership of the so-called Lady Führer, Gertrude Sholtz-Klink, the director of the Nazi Women's Bureau. In an interview in 1981, Klink expressed having no remorse for her contributing role but instead continued to serve up praise for the defeated Nazi Reich, extolling what she considered to be its enduring virtues, her interviewer informs us.[47]

Inasmuch as these women were for the most part not involved directly in planning or perpetrating atrocities (although a sizable number were),[48] these women are at least morally culpable for the role they played, even though some were more actively involved than others in the indoctrination and persecution process. In brief, mere membership in this Nazi booster club, despite that as individuals some members were more active than others in furthering the group's goals, implicates all members of the group collectively, even if some members accommodated only minimally the demands of group service and did nothing illegal or flagrantly immoral themselves in the process. Again, this is a case of 'passive' contribution to the Nazi atrocities. In this matter, I disagree with the view that women were "relatively powerless and de-politicized then" and "would certainly have to be considered *less* responsible than men" for Nazi genocide.[49]

Another case engenders the issue of the periphery of responsibility because its troubling nature is concerned with the Jewish *kapos,* or overseers, at Nazi concentration camps. Surely the Jews were the principal victims of Nazi terror. Nevertheless, some Jews were selected or volunteered to be SS or Gestapo collaborators in order to make things less difficult for themselves and perhaps to save their own lives—at least provisionally. One such tragic case (of 300 or more Jewish *kapos*) involved Jacob Tannenbaum, a pious Jew and the only survivor from a twelve-member family, who settled in the United States where he lived an exemplary postwar life. The American Justice Department's OSI, in a move that ignited some serious controversy (and soul-searching), accused Tannenbaum in 1987 of wartime atrocities. Neal Sher, director of the OSI, in justification of the OSI's only instance of prosecution of a Jewish *kapo*, claimed that Tannenbaum's case was significantly different from the others because he "engaged in physical violence against inmates." (See note 50.) Tannenbaum himself is reported to have suffered the loss of an eye and a serious back injury when he was beaten by Nazi personnel prior to the beatings he was accused of having inflicted on his own people in his role as a camp *kapo*.

For the Jewish collaborationist *kapos*, the line is crossed to victimizer with justiciable and moral responsibility when physical violence is used to brutalize camp inmates, despite instances where most *kapos* may have performed (or refused to perform) acts that thwarted or deferred Nazi designs. In other words, "the roles of victim and victimizer need not be mutually exclusive."[50] The problem for a law-respecting and ideally moral society is how to deal officially with these kinds of individuals.

The personal motives of Jewish *kapos* may be expected to differ in kind from other *kapos* and Nazi personnel, but this is a consideration that should not, and did not, militate against prosecution because the acts of physical violence and injuries to victims were the same, irrespective of the motives of the perpetrators. However, motives should count in the assessment of punishment on conviction as a possible mitigating factor. Of course, the likely defense in the case of the Jewish *kapos* is that, in the absence of their mediational role, the Nazis would have treated their captives even worse than the *kapos* did. (Other defenses have included "mistaken identity," "denial," "coercion," and the seemingly omnipresent "following orders.") And incidentally, this defense was the same defense claim made by some Nazi bigwigs, i.e., that they executed murderous policies in order to stave off even worse acts of persecution by Nazis more vicious than they were. In short, they cast themselves in the spurious role of the "lesser of evils."

In rebuttal, it is impossible to imagine how the lives of camp prisoners could have been made significantly, or even palpably, easier if it were not for the *kapos'* intercession, since their lives were fraught in any case with dispossession, imprisonment, humiliation, brutalization, and in most cases, death. Indeed, the Nazis often construed noncooperation by their Jewish captives as active defiance. In such instances, the Nazis punished their victims by murdering a disproportionate number of other Jews, according to eyewitness accounts at the Eichmann trial.[51] Witnesses to 'less evil being done' by *kapos* are as rare as the acts of kindness themselves reportedly were. In Tannenbaum's case, he admitted to Judge I. Leo Glasser, the judge who handled the Tannenbaum case, that he had beaten other inmates even when the Nazi guards were not present.[52] This admission suggests that he took his task more seriously than might be expected of a coercee or involuntary, 'passive' contributor. Moreover, his acts were criminal in nature. Therefore, he was rightly made justiciably accountable, a victimizer who was a perpetrator of Nazi persecution. The fact that he belonged to a people who were the main targets of the Nazis is a factor in deciding on a penalty; it does not diminish his role in persecution.

The "periphery of responsibility" question I have been discussing would be even more distressing and tragic in the case of the Jewish *kapo* if it were not for the fact that he committed serious crimes of persecution against innocent people. Neither Tannenbaum's mindset, nor that of the other Jewish *kapos*, could be expected to have been forged by the popular belief in the "dangerous inferiority of the Jewish race." Hence as a Jew, he could not dissociate himself from the Jewish identity of his victims,[53] thus in all likelihood making his actions seem to him to be selfish and unethical (to save his own skin). In other words, he did not have the dubious "advantage" of victimizing people with whom he did not share a personal identity. In the end, his health was in serious decline, so Tannenbaum's guilty plea before trial to every allegation against him resulted in a settlement, officially called a Consent Judgment of Denaturalization (because he fraudulently and illegally concealed his criminal behavior in his application for citizenship), an order signed and dated February 4, 1988, that canceled his citizenship.[54] He died soon thereafter.

In what sense, then, can we attribute responsibility for Nazi atrocities to *kapos* other than those, like Tannenbaum, who committed specific crimes? After all, under general threat of harm, the *kapos* in most cases dutifully served the Nazis in maintaining "order" among the captives. And yet, there are eyewitness accounts of some *kapos* performing (infrequently) acts of kindness and of the subtle subversion of the "order" imposed by the Nazi camp officials. I think that the key to a proper understanding of the contributory nature of the service provided by Jewish *kapos* to the Nazi cause must be found generally in the greater circumstantial context of the personal decision each made to become a *kapo*. In this respect, they are to be distinguished from Jews who refused to serve and those who were never compelled to serve under threat of harm. Those who refused to serve must be regarded as part of the Resistance, no matter what individual motives may have been operative, since "heroism is not a moral requirement." In other words, morality does not demand heroic proportions of courage when the only available option against complicity is self-sacrifice. The process of selecting Jewish agents of Nazi oppression (the *kapo*, the Jewish police, and so on), according to a credible account, had a veneer of voluntariness among Jewish candidates but, on closer inspection, it appears that individuals who volunteered did so with a sufficiently strong dose of fear and dread of consequences for not doing so.[55] Yet their actions were in the service of the Nazi program, despite their individual attitudes; and to this degree, they must be judged by their persecutory actions, which I believe opens them to the indictment of legal and moral responsibility. For, if we deny that all those who were variously compelled to serve the Nazi regime (and not only those who believed in the Nazi cause) are to be excused on that account alone, no one would be blamable, which is absurd, because everyone, including most of the worst offenders, would seek refuge in the "coercion" (or "following orders") defense. Thus we must ultimately distinguish between those people who consciously served the regime and those who deliberately thwarted it. *Kapos* who 'passively' served the Nazis but who did not do physical harm personally to others are responsible but not to the same extent as those who actively persecuted the camp inmates. Generally, the Jewish *kapos,* Jewish police, and Jewish councils instituted by the Nazis may have cooperated in varying degrees with their persecutors, but they were not the principle cause of their own victimization, despite the role they played in their own destruction.[56] Blaming the victims for their own destruction in this case is a mistake unless they knowingly contributed to or assisted in contributing to acts of persecution.

*Passive Contributor to
the Process of Victimization*

To return to consideration of the responsibility of millions of ordinary citizens associated with the Nazi Women's Bureau, at least one thing is clear. No member can be regarded as or presumed 'innocent' in the same way members of the Resistance or female nonmembers (especially so-called "apolitical" ones) were. There may have been many members of the bureau who did not actually commit or encourage, aid, and abet persecution, nor was the bureau ever condemned as a criminal organization (as a number of others had been). Therefore, the best way to characterize the responsibility of all bureau members is to distinguish between 'active' and 'passive' contributions to victimization and not only between victimizer and victim, because membership in a Nazi booster club is an unequivocal expression of one's commitment to its values and goals. Therefore, all members of the Bureau must be classified as being, to some degree, victimizers, albeit 'passive' contributors (with the exception of active participants in acts of persecution). Generally speaking, since many women had not joined the bureau, they cannot be accused of responsibility as individuals unless, and until, damning evidence can be obtained that implicates specific individuals in acts of persecution or in support of such acts.

A MODEL OF RESPONSIBILITY

Of the number of theories or models of responsibility one may adopt for classifying victimizers and nonvictimizers, the most persuasive is what one philosopher has called an "actual-sequence" model of responsibility, "a model that focuses on the actual sequence of events leading to behavior."[57] The virtue of this model, in my opinion, is that victimizers may be identified in terms of the type and degree of proximity to the causal chain of events with a persecutory outcome. However, some causes of persecution are not always morally responsible for specific acts committed. In this way, victimizers may "let things happen," i.e., they do nothing to discourage nor prevent bad things from happening; or they may "make things happen" by doing something to cause an expected persecutory outcome. It may be asked: In what sense does "letting things happen" or doing nothing to discourage or prevent a certain outcome "cause" or make one responsible for the outcome? Again, heroism and deliberate acts of self-sacrifice are not invariant features of morality. Therefore, to satisfy my minimalist notion of responsibility in this sense, 'doing nothing' becomes a cause in instances where universal standards of common decency or kindness or morality or simple justice would be expected to require at least some minimal show of sincere disapproval. Hence, using this standard, membership in a Nazi organization would, on its face, discredit any claim to sincere disapproval of any of the aims of the organization, including its broader role and function within Nazi society. A passive (and causal) contribution to persecution occurs, then, when a universal normative expectation of individual disapproval goes unfulfilled, short of heroism and courage, even if the outcome would not be altered or affected by the individual's most heroic or courageous act of resistance or sabotage. Because it is in this way that even tacit approval by a majority of people creates a pervasive climate of opinion that conduces to or encourages and supports the extreme instances of immoral and illegal behavior that characterized Nazi society.

In summary, an individual is a victimizer not only when he or she actively participates in an act of persecution or actively supports those who do, but also when an individual gives no indication that he or she may disapprove of the offense to universal standards. The latter can be regarded as a 'cause' of persecution in the sense that it promotes a permissive climate of opinion. Accordingly, people who are antisemites cannot free themselves from moral and perhaps legal responsibility for Nazi persecution on the ground that they did not do anything wrong. Their responsibility is rooted in their beliefs, which nourish the climate of insensitivity. In terms of a persecutory act, the 'nondoing' believer is a passive contributor to persecution. The victimizer who is a passive contributor to persecution may not have committed any specific act that constitutes or promotes a specific justiciable or immoral offense(s), but the victimizer's responsibility ought to extend even to such peripheral cases as the German antisemites who may personally disavow acts of cruelty by themselves or others against the persecuted. In this case, the degree of causal proximity to the outcome of persecution and atrocities may be more remote than the antisemite who welcomes persecution by others against Jews—some may even say too remote to be considered a link in a causal sequence; but I think one should not discount the importance of public opinion and of a popular climate of receptivity to persecution, because in the longer run this climate encourages and sustains—causes—the direct sequence of events that lead to or constitute persecution and extermination. In my opinion, this is the centerpiece of the legacy of the Nazi Holocaust. Therefore, the share of responsibility must distribute to the holders of antisemitic beliefs whose nature is consistent with or promotive of acts of persecution. For if the post-Holocaust generation can be said to have learned anything of moral consequence, it is that a society that tolerates or encourages antisemitism and racism can become a society that under the right mix of conditions promotes acts of persecution, pogroms, and genocide.

On the "actual-sequence" model of responsibility, the closer an individual's behavior comes to the actual sequence of events directly causing the offense, the more the perpetrator is subject to moral blame and perhaps legal prosecution, unless some important explanation or excuse removes him or her from blameworthiness for some (in-)action, e.g., proven insanity or coercion in the strictest sense. The latter might refer to a situation where a person, viz., a *kapo*, was an unwilling or forced instrument of SS violence.[58] In this situation, the individual lacks any autonomy or control over his own behavior, and so has no responsibility for his persecutory behavior. "No responsibility," "diminished responsibility," or "full responsibility" over one's behavior are categories that are calculable most clearly in the case of coercion. That is, there must be physical force applied or a direct and believable threat of extreme pain or threat to the life of the perpetrator used to induce the performance of the illegal or immoral action, i.e., a case of genuine coercion is a non-responsible cause of persecution nevertheless and not a threat addressed generally to those who fail to comply with the wishes or commands of the SS, inasmuch as there may be a standard, non-life-threatening response (i.e., one where a *kapo* need not brutalize his victims). On the other end of the 'responsibility' continuum is the 'active' contributor, victimizer, and persecutor who is fully responsible for his own and perhaps for others' acts of persecution.

COERCION AND DIMINISHED RESPONSIBILITY

An excuse of demonstrable coercion is ordinarily sufficient to diminish, or remove one from, blame. But if the Nazi victimizer assisted in persecution by collaborating or cooperating with the Nazis, and therefore exercised some degree of voluntariness in compliance with Nazi wishes or commands, he or she is rightly accused of actively contributing to Nazi atrocities and so may be justiciably responsible for war crimes. In showing unusual brutality and enthusiasm for one's persecutory task, no matter what the reason, particularly as there are cases of other *kapos* who did not do so, these victimizers may be seen as subverting any claim to diminished responsibility. Therefore, the perpetrator is more an active contributor to persecution. In the instance of a Jewish *kapo*, he was both victim and victimizer: As a Jew he was held captive in a Nazi labor or death camp and compelled to choose to collaborate and serve the enemies of his people while simultaneously persecuting his people with unusual brutality. The dual role of the Jewish *kapo* should not be construed as an argument against prosecution but rather as an important consideration in assessing penalty on conviction.

It may be argued, then, that the further away one or one's behavior is from the "actual-sequence" of offending events, the less justification there is for holding one legally or morally responsible for it. Nevertheless, one may actively participate in activities or events that encourage a climate of opinion that invites the sorts of offending behaviors and roles that are clearly blameworthy, such as the 'duties' and attitudes of the members of the Nazi Women's Bureau. I prefer to classify these Nazi women as active contributors to a climate of opinion that nourished, facilitated—and certainly did not detract from or undermine—the Nazi Holocaust and the commission of war crimes. But most were passive contributors to the Holocaust when seen from the viewpoint of their role in the Nazis' commission of war crimes and crimes against humanity. These women are morally responsible, if not legally blameworthy, for Nazi atrocities, because they expressed support for Nazism, especially since many German women did not join or refused to join the Women's Bureau—a point that must be included in any final reckoning about the plausibility of the charge of "collective guilt" against the German people. When is a 'failure to act' against persecution a determinate cause of the Nazis' atrocities? Could it be considered a passive contribution?

In what sense, then, is the expression "passive contributor" to be used, since nonactivists were not necessarily opposed to Nazi atrocities (e.g., they may have preferred to restrict their involvement to more subtle or indirect modes of support)? Jaspers defines "passivity" (as a form of blameworthy responsibility) in terms of remaining inactive when confronted with a surrounding environment saturated with "race mania," "delusions of a nationalistic revival based on fraud," and an inclination to wink "at the crimes then already committed."[59] In general, legal guilt typically involves actively doing something that is criminal, e.g., planning, aiding or abetting, and actually performing the illegal deeds, whereas passive guilt is not usually a justiciable offense (though some legal jurisdictions may regard it as a form a negligence in certain circumstances).[60] Passive guilt more likely involves, as Jaspers observes, some failure or "neglect to act whenever possible, to shield the imperiled, to relieve wrong, to countervail."[61] But lest heroism become the standard of morality, survival during periods of serious social insensitivities, cruelties, and depravity may require acquiescence in or flight from not only mass persecutions and murder but from the general social climate in which these evils are commonplace occurrences. "Passive" contribution to evil does not mean merely reluctant compliance to the forces of evil (what Jaspers calls "running with the pack"), which in effect becomes active contribution; rather it refers to the moral blameworthiness that accrues to "blindness for the misfortune of others, lack of imagination of the heart, inner indifference toward the witnessed evil."[62]

In other words, the mere fact that there were actual instances of "righteous" behavior that placed individuals at risk for their own family's safety and life, though heroism is not usually a requirement of moral goodness, are not simply 'heroic,' but they serve to show or exemplify what was possible with the presence of sufficient goodwill and moral commitment. In brief, the actions of the "righteous," as few or as subtle as they may have been, cast a certain 'moral' shadow over the majority of others who did nothing affirming of good in the face of evil.[63] It is in this context of Nazi society that the issue of "passive" contribution emerges and is to be understood. Although morality may not demand heroic actions in a climate of cruelty, as noted above, it may move some to heroism. In any case, the mere existence of the demonstrable possibility of opposition to evil, no matter how insufficient or subtle, places the burden of moral justification or excuse on those who apparently acquiesced in or did nothing to confront evil in light of the range of responses that were possible.

RESISTANCE AND THE ISSUE OF "COLLECTIVE GUILT"

There were, however, some told and, surely, untold instances of resistance and opposition to Nazi atrocities—but not enough. An account of the kinds and scope of resistance will shed some light on the suitability of a "collective guilt" indictment. Although it is tempting to conclude that the "collective guilt" charge is well earned owing to the widespread and overall favorable reception the Nazi regime received throughout its hold on power both in Germany and in other Nazi-controlled states, excluding those who actively and unequivocally opposed or resisted the genocidal policies of their respective states, a more tempered assessment is necessary in view of individual acts of resistance and avoidance of unjust accusation. Therefore, in building a case for continuing to pursue those living Nazis who were responsible, 'guilt' must be strictly construed as meaning 'justiciable' or 'punishable' guilt, i.e., where official investigation gathers the evidence, which is then fairly presented in a duly constituted and appropriate court of law, and where it is both sufficient to support prosecution and to legally justify conviction and punishment. This guilt is individual, and not collective, guilt and so must be treated in an individual case-by-case manner. Even a designated 'criminal' organization has members who would be tried on an individual basis. In this sense, "collective guilt" is an offense to legal justice. In addition, a view of moral responsibility that I used earlier in this chapter appears to give adequate refutation to the common claim that it was the (Nazi) system and its leaders who coerced every participant into making the active or passive contributions that they did, that is, that the contributors could not have done otherwise, because what they did, or failed to do, was beyond their own control.

However, the seriousness of a charge of "collective guilt" is underscored when sufficient evidence is available that indicates how truly infrequent and ineffective—and how small in numbers of people— instances of resistance and conspiracy against the Nazi atrocities, especially among the non-Jews, church officials, military personnel, politicians, and professionals, really were. Certainly, resistance may assume different forms, sometimes subtle and imperceptible. Yet any repugnance to war crimes and the Holocaust by Germans must not underrate the role played by the millions of bystanders and enthusiastic supporters (in their varying degrees) of Nazism; nor must any account of Nazi atrocities underplay "the importance as well of its tens of thousands of functionaries and willing perpetrators, and of the passivity and sometimes encouragement of the majority of legal and medical professional communities. Indeed, the long and deep-rooted history of German antisemitism, coupled with the circumstantial and popular need to cast blame for Germany's misfortunes on a ready-made 'scapegoat'," the Jews, must be included in the fullest account. "Accordingly, these form in large measure the basis on which popular receptivity existed to the legalization of repressive discrimination against the Jews and the widespread passivity, acceptance and 'denial' that accompanied the Final Solution to the Jewish Question."[64]

In a book about resistance to Hitler from within the Third Reich, the author cites "different sources and types of opposition to Nazi policies, strategies and activities"[65] and notes "a study which cites about 3,000 cases where 'ordinary' Germans tried to help the persecuted Jews. *Three thousand* courageous and righteous souls in a country of many millions of people! Although a concept of "collective guilt" may not be immune from criticism, it is even less warranted to discount the role of the vast majority of the German people in tolerating or contributing to the evils perpetrated by the Nazis."[66] Strictly speaking, however, I assume that there is no such entity as a 'German People' with a fixed national character that is present in each and every member of the German nation. For if there were, it would be easier to spread blame over an entire people.

But in my opinion, the principal argument against "collective guilt"—i.e., against ascribing guilt to the German people (or to any people) as a whole despite the overwhelming and pervasive support for the Nazi Reich in Germany, Austria, and elsewhere—is that there *are* obvious examples of individuals who put their own lives at risk—or were sacrificed for—hiding, feeding, and sheltering Jews. The well-known story of Anne Frank and the non-Jewish family who protected her is but one of many such occurrences.[67] Another is the case of Raoul Wallenberg, the Swedish diplomat whose heroic actions saved thousands of Hungarian Jews from the Nazis but eventually cost him his life at the hands of the advancing Soviet army and of those who incarcerated him.[68] In fact, the Israeli government under the auspices of Yad Vashem, the Holocaust Memorial in Israel, has recognized hundreds of "righteous gentiles" whose acts of resistance to the Holocaust helped save many thousands of Jewish lives. For instance, in spite of the antisemitism that has pervaded Poland for centuries, Yad Vashem in Israel has an "incomplete list of Poles executed for sheltering Jews" that contains the names of 521 Polish families. Moreover, "a number of fighters in the Polish underground army were killed or wounded as they tried to help the fighters of the Warsaw ghetto."[69] Other documented instances in which non-Jews rescued Jews include those of Anna Shimaite, a Lithuanian librarian, who saved "dozens of Jewish children from the Vilna ghetto"; Oskar Schindler, the Czech-German industrialist, who "spent a fortune to rescue from SS selection some 1,200 Jews working under his supervision in Poland"[70]; and André Trocmé, a Protestant minister, who with his wife and children, "the members of their church, and nearly all the citizens of Le Chambon-sur-Lignon" fed, hid, and "whenever possible spirited across the Swiss border by cooperating Christians" the German Jews or other victims of Nazis who came to them for help.[71]

In other words, these documented exceptions to the massive popular support for Nazi rule should remind us of the inherent injustice and logical error involved in indiscriminately casting blame for atrocities over an entire people(s) or ascribing to a people a certain character invariably present in all its members equally. The injustice done is 'blaming the innocent,' though there are some people, even in professional philosophy circles who believe that blaming and punishing the innocent is not always wrong, immoral, or unjust (e.g., Jeremy Bentham and some other utilitarians).[72] Given that there are different types and degrees of guilt, it is my view that only individuals, not peoples, can be blamed for their intentions, behaviors, or roles played, since only individuals are capable of these mental or physical actions. This defining characteristic is the reason that the search for a national character or the character of a people has always been foredoomed. In the context of 'blaming others,' which is what "collective guilt" involves, blame is either deserved or undeserved. To deserve blame, the accused must be shown, by the informed accuser, in some proper public forum for that purpose, on the basis of sound and sufficient evidence to have done or intended to do the sorts of things deserving of condemnation. Only then can 'guilt' be established on an individual basis with respect to intentions, actions, and roles and the type and extent to which each of these contributed to the individual's wrong-doing be determined. Nazi pursuer S. Wiesenthal invited a former Nazi official to the wedding of his daughter, explaining that his rescue by two Nazis (one the invitee; the other was eventually killed in battle) shows that [they] "are living proof, that it was possible to survive the Third Reich with clean hands," even if one was a Nazi.[73]

The accusation of "collective guilt" overwhelms the individual members of a presumed collectivity and forecloses any option of a defense since no proper public forum is possible for an individual to exculpate himself or herself, nor even if it were a practical possibility to put a nation on trial would the outcome justify the charge, since no individual or group can be authorized to speak for the people. In addition, "collective guilt" under-mines respect for or confidence in our concept of the rule of law because it burdens the accused and to prove innocence rather than the accuser to prove the guilt of the accused. Punishing the innocent is patently unjust. But not punishing or not even prosecuting the guilty is an even worse injustice.

A 'people' is in a basic sense an abstraction. Since a 'people' cannot speak for itself or act to defend itself, and since no individual or aggre-gate can be properly said to be its voice, moral and legal responsibility can be judged only on an individualized basis. Jaspers has drawn a disquieting parallel. About antisemitism he says: "A world opinion which condemns a people collectively is of a kind with the fact that for thousands of years men have thought and said, 'The Jews are guilty of the crucifixion.' Who are 'the Jews'? A certain minority group of religious and political zealots whose relative power among the Jews of that time, in cooperation with the Roman occupation authorities, led to the execution of Jesus."[74] Therefore, traditional Christian theology and the teachings of various Christian churches that blamed or continue to blame a people called "the Jews" for killing Jesus are subject to the same sorts of criti-cisms I noted previously with respect to the charge of "collective guilt" against "the Germans," "the Poles," or "the Ukrainians."

HOW TO DEAL WITH
THE ISSUE OF "COLLECTIVE GUILT"

However, it defies a common sense of justice to believe that a nation(s) that embraced so passionately and thoroughly the ideals and many nefarious practices of the Nazis and that subjected the world to so much evil consists of an aggregate of presumably innocent people who were either bystanders, resisters, or merely uninformed—until proven otherwise. As the Nazi period becomes more and more remote, the question of responsibility, including the fixing of blame and guilt, must be confronted boldly, not the least because of efforts by some historians to rewrite and distort, if not outright falsify, the past. A sketch of who was responsible and why so many people must share at least some moral responsibility for the Nazi persecutions and atrocities is necessary for historical explanation and understanding. However, justiciable blame and guilt must be filtered through a fair and appropriate judicial process on an individual-by-individual basis. Punishment, atonement, and forgiveness are also to be reckoned with on an individualized basis. However, the political, church, business, and professional leaders of Germany, Austria, Poland, and elsewhere have a special political responsibility in the wake of the Holocaust: to mold a cultural climate of opinion that respects and teaches the truth about their Nazi past, to accept general responsibility in both word and deed for the past wrongdoings, to make amends to surviving victims and their families (which some governments have done in some measure), and to support and vigorously defend the prosecution of remaining Nazi war criminals. To do any less will continue to raise the specter of "collective guilt" under which future generations will surely be judged: It will naturally reflect poorly on and the world will continue to be suspicious of all individuals who happen to be German, Polish, Austrian, and so on. The minimal demand of moral and legal responsibility is addressed to the leaders of these societies and to the popular opinion that usually motivates them: Show how repugnant the crimes committed by the Nazis and their collaborators were in view of the humane ideals of civilized society.

Individual members of society must also convincingly repudiate the Nazi past by rejecting antisemitism and educating society about the evils of "Nazi" society. The most tangible way this can be done is at the very least to demonstrate that the acceptance or toleration of the victimizers living out their twilight years without legal accountability mocks the ideals of legal justice and morality that we purport to cherish. In this limited sense, the question of responsibility is a methodological one, a call to action, because it requires a careful and determined officially sponsored and promoted effort to connect specific wrongdoings by individuals or groups of individuals to the configuration of circumstances in which they were done. Otherwise "collective guilt" is an unendurable onus placed on the aggregate of individuals and becomes, in effect, an arbitrary persecution of individuals in the name of the collectivity.

Accordingly, to subject the accused individuals to a fair judicial process is what distinguishes our concept of the rule of law from Nazi justice. Another major weakness of "collective responsibility" is that it blurs the distinction between victimizer and victim and between the generation of original Nazis and future generations of Germans, Austrians, and others who welcomed Nazism. For to hold all responsible, in effect, holds none responsible since it permits specific individuals to excuse their actions under Nazi rule by blaming the Nazi system as a whole and its agencies, asserting that they were coerced or duped into performing uncivilized deeds, i.e., it was beyond the control of individuals to prevent persecutions and atrocities.

The concept of the rule of law sketched previously is designed to identify arbitrary judgment in matters concerning relations among citizens, and between citizens and governments. Legal liability for wrongdoing must be established, and *criminal* liability can only be ascertained on an *individual,* and not a collective, basis. In prosecuting the criminals who were responsible for the Nazi persecutions, 'guilt' must be strictly construed here as 'punishable' guilt in accord with the provision of law, where the evidence justifies prosecution, conviction, and punishment. Moral responsibility on the other hand, is different. Since so many millions of people—the overwhelming majority of Germans and Austrians—welcomed Nazi rule, as I have stressed, and since the evil that the Nazis did was so widespread and met with minimal resistance from the ranks of the Nazified masses, a collective moral indictment is absolutely appropriate but it must be understood in a special sense.

My own position on the question of ascribing collective moral responsibility for the Holocaust to the German people is, ultimately, one of principle, viz., *individualized* proof of complicity in persecution and in fostering a climate of racial and religious hatred is essential. This position accords well with Jasper's argument that "there can be no collective moral guilt of a people or a group within a people" because "a people" and "a group" lack the distinctive moral qualities and conditions that characterize "individuals," such as possession of a conscience, a free will, and a capacity to reason.[75] Nevertheless, I do believe that a highly qualified sense of "collective responsibility" makes sense, but I will support this claim in due course.

A polar opposition to my own view, despite a certain powerful emotional strain of sympathy I may have for his outrage, is found in Dershowitz's assertion that the Germans bear collective responsibility "for the crimes of their leaders—whom they elected and enthusiastically supported and whose mass murders were carried out with the assistance and know-ledge of so many citizens." Further, he regards "the rebuilding of postwar Germany into one of the world's most affluent nations" as "a moral disgrace." The German people, collectively, should have been made to suffer a generation of poverty, with exceptions being made "for those who opposed Nazism."[76] (Of course, the former East Germany was made to suffer the burden of an impoverishing Communist rule.) A more moderate answer to the question of collective German responsibility for Nazi atrocities has been proposed by A. Zvie Bar-On. Bar-On gives a qualified affirmation to the charge, which is intended to avoid the blurring of distinctions between victims and victimizers and between the worst war crimes offenders and those who stood on the sidelines, inactively and silently. Bar-On asserts:

> We plead for an exceptional application [of collective guilt] in our case because of the entirely exceptional character of the crime, namely, (a) the initiation, planning, and execution of the genocide of the Jewish people. . . (b) the transformation . . . of the German state, all its economic, juridical, and technical resources included into a criminal state. . . . The crime is exceptional, entirely new, without precedent in the history of mankind, and this fact justifies the use of the concept of collective guilt when trying to measure the responsibility for the crime.[77]

Yet this position, too, appears to punish the innocent along with the guilty.

AGAINST "COLLECTIVE GUILT"

In the final analysis, I think both arguments for collective guilt must fail in view of justice because they necessarily presume the individualized guilt of all German people, distributively, as a practical consequence of a collective attribution of blame, and certainly this is an unjustly deserved stigma on those who were clearly and demonstrably innocent. However, Jaspers' position is too simplistic and belies the fact that the Holocaust could have been carried out only with the active assistance of many in the German population, even as many more segments of the population cheered them on or at the very least feigned ignorance about the deporta-tions and mass murder. In any case, fairness requires that we note that some (but very few) actively opposed the policies and actions of the Nazi government. A few people resisted overtly, others did so with great subtlety; and some were undoubtedly coercively compelled to commit acts of (or in support of) persecution. I would object to the charge of collective guilt that would wrongly tarnish those who fall into these categories. And what about the children of the Nazi generation who were nurtured in the cultural milieu of hatred, intolerance, passionate nationalism, and militarism? Are they, too, morally responsible, even in a minimalist sense (the perpetrators being most responsible), especially in view of the fact that they are now in control of a prosperous and united, democratic Germany? Are future generations of Germans to carry the stigma of collective liability? My response is somewhat different from the views of others I have cited.

IN SUPPORT OF
A QUALIFIED "COLLECTIVE RESPONSIBILITY"

I believe that collective moral responsibility is appropriate but only in the abstract, nondistributive sense[78] that as a consequence of the Holocaust Germany's social institutions and its leadership generally are morally required to confront their Nazi past, since a certain generalized suspicion will probably always pervade the world community about the widespread complicity of most Germans in Nazi crimes. But because Germany's population during the era of the Third Reich so widely welcomed Nazism with its overtly antidemocratic and antisemitic character and goals, Germans (distributively) today are collectively responsible for squarely facing Germany's Nazi past by: (1) educating their citizenry, particularly the young, about what happened; (2) educating their people—unambiguously and with conviction—about the repulsive evil of antisemitism, including its theological Christian roots; (3) educating their people about the pernicious nature of claims to racial superiority and of extreme and pretentious forms of German nationalism and its ever-present component of xenophobia; (4) principled opposition to extremist groups, repudiating their messages of hate; (5) supporting the continued prosecutions of Nazi persecutors; and finally, (6) educating Germans about the enduring virtues of democratic pluralism and the principle of toleration and acceptance of national, ethnic, racial, and religious differences. Accordingly, if German society (collectively) through its institutions and leadership today does not vigorously and clearly support each of these six items, I believe that the ascription of collective responsibility becomes increasingly plausible. Furthermore, each individual German, especially of the post-Nazi generation, must accept in a non-subtle manner the six items and show his or her support for them. For example, as one observer of Germany's record of war crimes trials has indicated: "In the children's generation, the distinction must be drawn between those who voice no criticisms but are ambivalent regarding the existence of such trials, and those who support and promote the continuation of the trials out of a sense of human, historical and political responsibility."[79] The subtlety inherent in this distinction raises the specter of suspicion of a cover-up by those of bad conscience or those who wish to evade Germany's responsibility, perhaps owing to their own or some family member's role in persecution.

The major point in holding a collectivity such as "the German people" responsible is that a special responsibility falls on each and every member of German society to demonstrably justify why as individuals they reject Germany's Nazi past and as well the sorts of parties, policies, actions, and attitudes that contributed to Hitler's Reich.[80] Of course, smaller organizations that are goal-oriented institutions like the People's Courts or formal collectivities like the Nazi party or any of its subgroups have an identity independent of the specific persons who may at any given time assume roles within the group. These collectivities "have a purpose, and members' performance is evaluated in relation to their contributions to that purpose.[81] The possibility of a moral assessment of individuals and collectivities, however, presupposes the legitimate application of external standards, i.e., moral standards that are external to the group, to its members' roles[82] and actions, and to the group's (internal) goals.

SUMMARY

In summary, the term 'responsibility' is intended as a broader category than (but including) justiciable blameworthiness and guilt. However, it is (and probably always was) impossible to determine at this late hour and in individual cases who disregarded or violated accepted and time-honored universal standards of decency, morality, and justice and when, in what ways, how often, and under what specific circumstances. What we know today we know for certain: The appeal of Nazism, particularly its antisemitic character, was widespread throughout Germany, Austria, and most Eastern European countries. Therefore, I believe it is fitting—not only in the special sense I have delineated—to ascribe moral responsibility to the 'collectivity' known as the German people. However, in the final analysis, moral accountability on the individual level must take place between the person and his conscience, the person and his god, and the person and his family (children and grandchildren) and between the older and younger generations, if the pervasive self-deception, denial, and concealment of the generation of Nazi persecutors can be overcome. But if current and future generations of Europeans and the others who sympathized with Nazism fail to assume "collective responsibility" (in the sense noted in the preceding section) for the deeds of the Nazi generation, the world's suspicions and fears that Nazi ideals and influence in

Germany may still be alive and well among the masses but underground only temporarily may be justified. I believe that the current generation of Germans must earnestly and convincingly dissociate itself from anti-semitism and the pernicious ideals of German supremacy and superiority. After all, the Germans as a people did not really suffer after the war, certainly not in the same way and to the same extent that they wrought suffering on those around them.

The Allied bombing of German cities, Communist rule in East Germany, and the war crimes trials are incommensurate with the government-sponsored atrocities the Nazis perpetrated on the Jewish people and other victims. Postwar reconstruction that has raised Germany to unparalleled economic power in Europe is hardly a "collective" penalty for Nazism, as Dershowitz has noted. Therefore, Germans today must educate themselves about what the Nazi generation did and reject it part and parcel. So much is necessary for beginning the process of "re-sanctification," if such is possible in human moral standing after Auschwitz. If not, the world's suspicions are regrettably well founded and collective moral blame for an inevitable emergence of a Fourth Reich will fall squarely on the shoulders of each and every German who does not or who refuses to dissociate himself or herself from the currents that make it possible.

NOTES

1. Robert Nozick, *The Examined Life: Philosophical Meditations* (New York: Simon and Schuster, 1989), pp. 238–39.

2. Richard L. Rubenstein, *After Auschwitz* (Indianapolis: Bobbs-Merrill, 1976), pp. 224–25.

3. Alice L. Eckardt and A. Roy Eckardt, *Long Night's Journey into Day: A Revised Retrospective on the Holocaust*, rev. ed. (Detroit: Wayne State University Press, 1988), pp. 16–72. The authors cite another prominent theologian, who writes: "The cornerstone of Christian anti-Semitism is the superseding or displacement myth . . . that the mission of the Jewish people was finished with the coming of Jesus Christ." The Eckardts concur: The murderous implications of this teaching were spelled out in the slaughter of "six million Jews by baptized Christians" (p. 71). See also Frank E. Manuel, *The Broken Staff: Judaism Through Christian Eyes* (Cambridge, Ma.: Harvard University Press, 1992).

4. See David S. Wyman, *The Abandonment of the Jews* (New York: Pantheon, 1985), pp. 290–307.

5. *New York Times*, September 5, 1991, p. 1.

6. "An Unpardonable Amnesty," *Newsweek*, September 16, 1991, p. 40.

7. "Historical revisionism" is the label often given to attempts by a few publicists to falsify history in the name of "open debate" and "free speech" in order to rekindle the fires of antisemitism.

8. Alan M. Dershowitz, *Chutzpah* (Boston: Little, Brown, 1991), p. 130.

9. Reported in *New York Times*, May 2, 1991, p. A7.

10. The two Germanys, the Netherlands, Yugoslavia, France, Canada, Australia, Poland, and others are listed in the *Encyclopedia of the Holocaust*, vol. 4 (New York: Macmillan, 1990), pp. 1504–18; also see Owen M. Kupferschmid and Ruti G. Teitel, "Legal Responses to the Holocaust: Issues in Jurisprudence and History," in Yehuda Bauer et al., eds., *Remembering for the Future*, vol. 2 (Oxford: Pergamon Press, 1989), p. 1272.

11. Thomas Buergenthal, *International Human Rights* (St. Paul: West, 1988), pp. 47–49.

12. See Kenneth C. Randall, "Universal Jurisdiction Under International Law," *Texas Law Review*, vol. 66, no. 4 (March 1988), p. 813; the communiqué was reported in Attorney-General v. Eichmann, *International Law Reports*, vol. 36, p. 59; cited by John M. Rogers, "Prosecuting Terrorists: When Does Apprehension in Violation of International Law Preclude Trial?" *University of Miami Law Review*, vol. 42, no. 2 (November 1987), p. 454, n. 38.

13. Hannah Arendt, *Eichmann in Jerusalem* (New York: Viking Press, 1966), p. 264.

14. See Naomi Roht-Arriaza, "State Responsibility to Investigate and Prosecute Grave Human Rights Violations in International Law," *California Law Review*, vol. 78 (1990), pp. 463–64.

15. James W. Moeller, "United States Treatment of Alleged Nazi War Criminals: International Law, Immigration Law, and the Need for International Cooperation," *Virginia Journal of International Law*, vol. 25 (Summer 1985), p. 857.

16. Ibid., p. 856; in fact, the 1991–1992 Noriega case makes the same point.

17. Buergenthal, *International Human Rights*, p. 50.

18. Steven Fogelson, "The Nuremberg Legacy: An Unfulfilled Promise," *Southern California Law Review*, vol. 63 (March 1990), pp. 884–85.

19. *In re* Extradition of Demjanjuk, 612F. Supp. 544, 556, 557 (1985).

20. Whitney R. Harris, *Tyranny on Trial* (Dallas: Southern Methodist University Press, 1970), p. 494.

21. Randall, "Universal Jurisdiction," p. 811.

22. Ibid., p. 814.

23. Ibid., p. 814.

24. Ibid., p. 812.

25. Eric S. Kobrick, "The Ex Post-Facto Prohibition and the Exercise of Universal Jurisdiction over International Crimes," *Columbia Law Review*, vol. 87 (November 1987), p. 1531.

26. Ibid.

27. *In re* Extradition of John Demjanjuk, Misc. no. 83–349, Memorandum Opinion and Order, p. 43. As of October 1992, Demjanjuk is appealing before the Israeli Supreme Court his conviction and death sentence by an Israeli court.

28. Ibid., p. 45.

29. Accord Attorney General v. Eichmann, *American Journal of International Law*, vol. 56, p. 833.

30. Judge Frank J. Battisti cites Shabtai Rosenne, "The Effect of Sovereignty on Municipal Law," *British Year Book of International Law*, vol. 27 (1950), pp. 267, 284–85.

31. *In re* Extradition of John Demjanjuk, p. 46; also this expresses the 'passive personality' and 'protective' principles of criminal jurisdiction as cited in Moeller, "Treatment of Alleged Nazi War Criminals," pp. 851–52.

32. These are, in part, some of the elements noted by legal expert Irwin Cotler in "Nazi War Crimes—International Responsibility," *Patterns of Prejudice,* vol. 20, no. 4 (1986), p. 33.

33. Cited by Allan Ryan, Jr., *Quiet Neighbors* (New York: Harcourt Brace Jovanovich, 1984), p. 205.

34. I paraphrase the words of legal scholar Stephen J. Massey, "Individual Responsibility for Assisting the Nazis in Persecuting Civilians," *Minnesota Law Review,* vol. 71, no. 1 (October 1986), p. 98.

35. 8 U.S.C. S 1251 (a)(19); this statute and the Laipenieks (1982) and Sprogis cases were cited by Massey, "Individual Responsibility."

36. Laipenieks v. INS., 750 f.2d 1427, 1432 (9th Cir. 1985). Laipenieks was a member of the Nazi-controlled Latvian Political Police.

37. United States v. Sprogis, 763 F.2d 115, 122–23 (2d Cir. 1985). Sprogis was a Latvian police official.

38. United States v. Kowalchuk, 571 F. Supp. 72, 81 (E. D. Pa. 1983); *cert. denied,* 1065. Ct. 1188 (1986). Cited by Massey, "Individual Responsibility." Kowalchuk was a member of the Nazi-controlled Ukrainian auxilliary police stationed in Poland, according to OSI's Ryan, *Quiet Neighbors,* pp. 269, 356.

39. United States v. Dercacz, 530 F. Supp. 1348, 1351 (E.D.N.Y. 1982). Cited in Massey, "Individual Responsibility." Dercacz was a member of the Ukrainian police in Lvov.

40. *New York Times,* August 1, 1991; also, Simon Wiesenthal, *Justice Not Vengeance* (New York: Grove Weidenfeld, 1989), p. 207.

41. Martin Heidegger, the philosophy professor, is a case in point. He became the first Nazi rector of the University of Freiburg in 1933. His passionate support for national socialism, with its antisemitic character, has become a topic of some serious academic interest since 1989. For example, see Tom Rockmore and Joseph Margolis, eds., *The Heidegger Case* (Philadelphia: Temple University Press, 1992); Günther Neske and Emil Kettering, *Martin Heidegger and National Socialism* (New York: Paragon House, 1990); Victor Farías, *Heidegger and Nazism* (Philadelphia: Temple University Press, 1989), p. 84, passim; also, Michael E. Zimmerman, "The Thorn in Heidegger's Side: The Question of National Socialism," *Philosophical Forum,* vol. 20, no. 4 (Summer 1989), especially pp. 353–58; Leon Stein, "The Holocaust and the Legacy of Existentialism," in Bauer et al., *Remembering for the Future,* vol. 2 (1989), p. 1946.

42. Richard L. Rubenstein and John K. Roth, *Approaches to Auschwitz* (Atlanta: John Knox Press, 1987), pp. 154, 229–53; also, see "Subsequent Nuremberg Proceedings," *Encyclopedia of the Holocaust,* vol. 4 (New York: Macmillan, 1990), pp. 1501–03.

43. John K. Roth, "On Losing Trust in the World," in A. Rosenberg and G. Myers, eds., *Echoes From the Holocaust*, (Philadelphia: Temple University Press, 1988), p. 170.

44. Arendt, *Eichmann in Jerusalem*, p. 287.

45. Jeffrey Reiman, *Justice and Modern Moral Philosophy* (New Haven: Yale University Press, 1990), p. 125.

46. Gerald L. Posner, *Hitler's Children* (New York: Random House, 1991), pp. 41–69.

47. See Claudia Koonz, *Mothers in the Fatherland* (New York: St. Martin's Press, 1987), pp. xvii–xxxv.

48. Although I do not know whether she was a member of the Nazi Women's Bureau, Hermine Braunsteiner-Ryan is a well-known war criminal who relinquished her U.S. citizenship in 1971 rather than endure a denaturalization hearing. Evidence of her active participation in the murders of thousands of Jews at the Maidanek death camp led to her eventual deportation from the United States to Germany, which tried and convicted her of murder in 1981. She is now serving a life sentence in Germany. See Ryan, *Quiet Neighbors*, pp. 46–52.

49. See Ronald Aronson, "Responsibility and Complicity," *Philosophical Papers*, vol. 19, no. 1 (1990), pp. 66, 72; he explores the broader question of degrees of responsibility from passivity to criminal liability.

50. *New York Times*, May 26, 1987; Sam Freedman wrote this article.

51. Abigail L. Rosenthal, "The Right Way to Act," in Rosenberg and Myers, *Echoes from the Holocaust*, pp. 155, 162.

52. I. Leo Glasser is the Federal Eastern District Court New York Judge.

53. Military training required a certain dehumanization of the enemy in order to block the soldiers' personal identification with his/her targets. Tannenbaum had no such self-deceptive psychological refuge.

54. *New York Times*, February 5, 1988; also, *Washington Post Magazine*, April 24, 1988.

55. David Altshuler and Lucy S. Davidowicz, *Hitler's War Against the Jews* (New York: Behrman House, 1978), pp. 122–23.

56. Ervin Staub, *The Roots of Evil* (New York: Cambridge University Press, 1989), pp. 31–32.

57. John Martin Fischer, "Introduction: Responsibility and Freedom," in John Martin Fischer, ed., *Moral Responsibility* (Ithaca: Cornell University Press, 1986), pp. 42, 53, 59.

58. For a description of this type of coercion, see my book, *Coercion and Autonomy* (Westport: Greenwood Press, 1986), pp. 38–39, passim.

59. Karl Jaspers, *The Question of German Guilt* (New York: Capricorn Books, 1961), p. 69.

60. For instance, Good Samaritan laws will impose criminal penalties for 'failure to help' in time of peril to others. See Hyman Gross, *A Theory of Criminal Justice* (New York: Oxford University Press, 1979), pp. 27–28.

61. Jaspers, *The Question of German Guilt*, p. 69.

62. Ibid., p. 70.

63. It has been said that even bystanders came to accept—and like—"the suffering of victims and the behavior of perpetrators" (Staub, *Roots of Evil*, pp. 82, 151–57).

64. These quotes are from my review of the book by Peter Hoffmann entitled *German Resistance to Hitler* (Cambridge: Harvard University Press, 1988); the review is found in *Holocaust and Genocide Studies*, vol. 4, no. 4 (1989), pp. 508–9.

65. Hoffman, *German Resistance to Hitler*, pp. 52–59.

66. Ibid., my review of Hoffmann's book, pp. 508–9.

67. *Anne Frank* (New York: Washington Square Press, 1972).

68. Harvey Rosenfeld, *Raoul Wallenberg: Angel of Rescue* (Buffalo: Prometheus, 1982), pp. 35–38.

69. Wiesenthal, *Justice Not Vengeance*, p. 216.

70. Cited by Richard Rubenstein and John K. Roth, *Approaches to Auschwitz*, p. 224.

71. Ibid., pp. 225–27.

72. For example, see Igor Primoratz, *Justifying Legal Punishment* (Atlantic Highlands: Humanities Press International, 1989), pp. 43, 44–65.

73. Wiesenthal, *Justice Not Vengeance*, pp. 9–10.

74. Jaspers, *The Question of German Guilt*, pp. 41–42.

75. Ibid., pp. 40, 42, 79.

76. Dershowitz, *Chutzpah*, p. 137.

77. A. Zvie Bar-On, "Measuring Responsibility," *Philosophical Forum*, vol. 16, no. 1-2 (Fall-Winter 1984–1985), pp. 106–7.

78. In brief, what may be true of German society *writ large* is not invariably true of each individual German. Peter A. French, "Morally Blaming Whole Populations," in V. Held, S. Morgenbesser, and T. Nagel, eds., *Philosophy, Morality and International Affairs* (New York: Oxford University Press, 1974), pp. 282–83.

79. Helge Grabitz, "Problems of Nazi Trials in the Federal Republic of Germany," *Holocaust and Genocide Studies*, vol. 3, no. 2 (1988), p. 210.

80. I believe that my argument avoids the criticism raised by individualists who believe that morally blaming collectivities like "the German people" is either unjust or meaningless. For a discussion of the differences between "aggregative" and "conglomerative" collectivities, see Peter A. French, "Types of Collectivities and Blame," *Personalist*, vol. 56 (1975), pp. 164–68.

81. Steven J. Massey, "Assistance in Persecution," *Minnesota Law Review*, 1986, p. 137.

82. As a noted theorist stresses, there is a link between role behavior and individual choice or acceptance. This link will justify a moral evaluation of a role within an organization. See, R. S. Downie, "Social Roles and Moral Responsibility," *Philosophy*, vol. 39, no. 147 (January 1964), p. 30.

7

THE REBUTTAL OF ARGUMENTS AGAINST PROSECUTION

THE "PASSAGE OF TIME" ARGUMENT

The main thrust of the "passage of time" argument is not altogether to deny responsibility for the Holocaust but to excuse the offenders from punishment and so from a burdensome, pointless prosecution for everyone concerned. The argument claims that too much time has elapsed—as of 1992, almost fifty years. This fact compels consideration of some crucial consequences and facets of the argument.

Since the 1940s, Nazi war criminals have fanned out over the globe, established new lives for themselves, and in many notorious cases assumed new identities. These people have, for the most part, assimilated into their host communities, raised families, lead productive lives, and stayed clear of politics—at least conspicuous politics. In some well-known cases, even their spouses were unaware of their past complicity, e.g., the Braunsteiner-Ryan case. To prosecute these people now, the argument goes, would disrupt if not destroy their well-established lives and those of their (innocent) families. Although it may be true that they should have been brought to trial almost fifty years ago, it did not happen; the war criminals who escaped detection and/or prosecution, so the argument goes, have earned the right to remain undisturbed. Besides, many persecutors have since died, and those who survive today are so old that they are surely no threat to society; they will die soon anyway. Also, as most of the potential witnesses against them have died, memories of those surviving victims have faded, and their tormentors have undergone body changes over the years, positive and unimpeachable identification, it is argued, is very nearly unobtainable.

And finally, there is a last variation on the "passage of time" argument. Efforts to prosecute the older generation of Nazi war criminals somehow make their offspring and others of the new generations feel responsible for the sins of their fathers and mothers. One unwanted consequence of this situation is that it begets a resentment and a new antagonism against Jewish people because these innocent parties feel unjustly victimized.

Many do not see themselves as inheritors of the gross evil done nor do they feel obligated to correct the 'wrongs' of the older generation (if indeed they even see these as 'wrongs'): They no longer wish to be made to feel guilty or responsible for what some other people at some other time did.[1] In fact, a prominent Berliner has observed that many resentful young Germans, fueled by the attitudes of many of the older Nazi generation, have begun to believe or encourage the sentiment that the continued existence of the Jewish people after Auschwitz represents a serious obstacle to the future resurrection of German national pride. The reason is that Jews will always bear witness—"eternal witness"—against the German people for the support they gave the Nazis in carrying through the murderous Holocaust against the Jewish people. This new form of antisemitism[2] (i.e., another reason to hate the Jews and to promote their persecution), already discernible in the reunified Germany, can be expected also to intensify sentiments against future prosecutions of Nazi war criminals and probably against further reparation payments to Nazi-era victims.

As an aside, my own reaction to this emerging phenomenon is that the haste of the "resentful young Germans" to bury the past ought to be accompanied by an equally passionate commitment to confront the current sources and manifestations of longstanding antisemitism, xenophobia, and the extreme forms of militaristic nationalism. It is simply not enough for them to appeal to Germany's democratic fed-eralism as if it were a permanent obstacle to any future authoritarian turn because the aforementioned evils of Germany's past will continue to corrode and destroy and to foredoom an untested future where Germany's economic prosperity may eventually evaporate. In other words, Germany's embrace of democracy may be proportionate to its economic successes. Moreover, to prematurely "bury the past" before fully confronting it (e.g., by prosecuting Nazi murderers, many of whom continue to draw healthy pensions) should be seen as a prelude to a re-writing of history and an evasion of responsibility in the name of national renewal.

The central points of the variations of the 'special pleading' argument as presented above are (1) that prosecution is pointless because of its disruptive effect on the innocent families of the offenders; (2) that in view of the offenders' productivity and trouble-free lives since the acts of crime, the risk of a possible trial and conviction would be a loss to the community of a currently and ostensibly law-abiding citizen; and (3) that the victimizers and their whitewashers will characterize themselves as the new "victims" of the Jews, another pernicious form of blaming the victim for his (their) victimization. However in response to this argument we must include *all* the factors, influencing a final accounting of the force of this 'passage of time' claim.

Chief among these neglected or suppressed factors is that the disruptiveness is caused not only by the state's prosecution but also by the deception that the offenders have allowed their families to endure and for which they are only now being called to account. The innocence of families is on its face uncontested; but family members are at least as much victims of deliberate deception as they are of the prosecution process. The burden for wrongdoing must again be shifted back to the wrongdoer and not placed on the prosecutor of criminals.

It is also important to realize that the initiation of a prosecution process for a suspected offender should not be viewed as a disruption of society in general. The survivors of Nazi persecution and the living relatives of those who perished may continue to seek legal redress by the civilized community for the crimes that were committed. There is no statute of limitations in international law or in the laws of many countries for these crimes within the lifetimes of the perpetrators.[3] Even those victims who prefer to let sleeping dogs lie rather than risk a revival and repetition of the Holocaust often have sentiments in serious need of moral satisfaction. They recognize that reasonable assurance cannot be given that Nazism won't reemerge even if prosecution occurs; thus there are many who do support bringing war criminals to justice. And they may argue persuasively that a span of almost fifty years is *not* sufficiently long to justify abandoning the reexamination of the issues or the prosecuting of the remaining offenders.

In this vein, a preferable action would be a legal and systematic prosecution process for war criminals. Any departure from such policy for war crimes or crimes against humanity should never be based on a consideration of time, as passage of time is irrelevant to the determination of criminal or moral responsibility. For if anything, extensive passage of time between the commission of war crime and its legal redress should be regarded as *borrowed* or privileged freedom and count against, not for, the 'war crime' defendant. Evasion of justice is never a moral defense or excuse. Sociopolitical and legal freedom are viewed in our society as rights and privileges ordinarily accorded to citizens who are respecters of law, not to those who violate it and subvert the institutions of civilized society. Furthermore, in the case of Nazi-related prosecutions, virtually all so far have been successful in demonstrating on the basis of sufficient evidence the identities of defendants. This fact is the main reason for discouraging the claim of the defense in the Demjanjuk case that "they have the wrong man"—a case of "mistaken identity."

THE "EXTENUATING CIRCUMSTANCES" ARGUMENT

The "extenuating circumstances" argument has a cluster of related themes, which appear either to diminish the severity of both criminal and moral wrongdoing or to excuse the wrongdoers from prosecution altogether and thence from punishment.

Although many Nazis admit to being guilty of participation in 'crimes against humanity,' 'war crimes,' and 'crimes against the peace,' some among them collaborated with or allowed themselves to be used by the victorious Allies, specifically the Americans, in the immediate postwar period. They not only disclosed hidden details about the Third Reich but also gave testimony against the Soviet Communists, whom the Americans came to regard as untrustworthy allies. Consequently, owing to the valuable service these Nazis provided, the argument goes, they should be shown leniency if not completely excused for the offense they had committed. In this regard, I cite the case against Arthur Rudolph that I discussed earlier.

Another 'extenuation' argument claims that Nazis are not fully responsible for their actions because the system of brutality and of threatened reprisals for noncompliance compelled them to do what they did. Thus the claim straddles the arguments of being excused (i.e., admittedly having done wrong but being coerced to do so) and being totally exculpated because self-preservation in the face of serious threats has been deemed the only natural and reasonable course of action.

The "Special Consideration" Argument

My response to the lead argument above is best outlined in a preinstitutional, moral context but with the use of a legal analogy. Again, it is noted that the final outcome of a legal proceeding is of less concern in this book than the issue of whether and on what grounds the suspected perpetrator should be brought to court. Hence the rebuttal, like the arguments themselves, will be decidedly less legal than sociopolitical and moral.

There is a common though questionable practice in U.S. criminal law called 'plea bargaining,' which is usually a prearraignment practice by which defense counsel convinces the prosecutor to "grant concessions in return for a guilty plea."[4] Just as it is possible to suppress some or all evidence against a defendant, depending on the circumstantial nature and severity of the offense and the jurisdiction in which the offense occurred, it is also possible that plea bargaining may not be sufferable under the circumstances. A serious capital crime is one for which the death penalty may be imposed. It is unlikely that a capital offense such as treason during wartime or the assassination of an important political figure will allow such plea bargaining since public outrage, public order and safety, and other superseding moral factors must be considered in deciding whether to indict and prosecute, as well as in determining the severity of punishment to be administered. A decision not to prosecute a capital offense would be generally regarded as a serious failure by a legal system in fulfilling one of its basic purposes: the stipulation of the essential obligations that citizens owe their community. Thus if the officers of a legal system were to tolerate a failure to discharge such an obligation, the morality and justice of the system would certainly be seriously vitiated, especially in a case of capital offense, which is clearly a flouting by the alleged criminal of a basic respect for the values of society, especially respect for law in general.

By analogy, if the officers of any system of law, international or national, were to fail to bring charges against those suspected of attacking that system at its foundation, the failure itself would become a serious subversion of that system. The main point of this argument is that not bringing an assumed offender through a prosecution process designed to account for wrongdoing is an undermining of the integrity of the social system. The sufficiency of evidence against an offender is the basis for the foregoing assumption. The claim being made here is not that all Nazi war criminals must be executed or even receive some punishment for their actions as the determination of guilt and punishment is decided in the legal process. The claim is that they must be brought to a public and open court so that the legal process may fulfill its purpose. Thus war criminals who may have helped the United States in the postwar anti-Communist scramble for position may be given lighter or no sentences, depending on the facts and other considerations in specific cases. But it would be morally indefensible, a harm to the civilized, moral community and its legal institutions, not to bring these persecutors before the appropriate court for these determinations to be made. However, I do think that a failure to punish in significant ways a convicted Nazi war criminal imposes the heaviest burden of justification on those parties who failed to do so.

It is a matter of the highest legal and moral consideration that any quid pro quo agreement between prosecution and defense, e.g., plea bargaining or not bringing charges, that diminishes the suspects' or defendants' likelihood of going to trial should take into account the character of the crime(s) in question. In short, excuses are morally defensible when admissible in relation to the degree of punishment and not, in my view, in determining whether an alleged war criminal should be prosecuted.

THE "DIMINISHMENT OF RESPONSIBILITY" ARGUMENT

An argument has been forwarded that the Nazi offenders were con-strained by the coercing agents of the Nazi system to persecute those individuals targeted by the Nazi party. An analysis of the meaning of coercion as applied in this context will demonstrate this argument to be argument *but only if* it can be defended in a particular instance. To use this argument in a blanket sense to apply to all suspects of Nazi war crimes in general would be a serious affront to the intrinsic indignation of a demo-cratic society regarding the heinous nature of the offenses in question. Further, the "diminishment of responsibility" argument indiscriminately applied presumes a theory of moral responsibility that sharply challenges democratic views by forwarding a concept of the individual whose will can be totally subverted as the mechanism of the "mind of the State."

As to the argument that the Nazi offenders were compelled by the coercing agents of the Nazi system to persecute those targeted by the Nazi party, it is clearly defeated both by a true grasp of the meaning of coercion and by the heinous nature of their offenses. A certain theory of moral responsibility (viz., the 'actual-sequence' model defined in Chapter 6) is presupposed in the following conception of coercion.

In general, the following definition of coercion is proposed: "Q is coerced by P when P causes Q to relinquish his or her known and valued autonomy over him- or herself in some limited respect, for example, over Q's (not) doing q by controlling Q's (not) doing q. This definition covers both physical and nonphysical types of coercion."[5] On the one hand, if Q is dominated by P in a total power relationship, Q (for action, q) becomes an extension of P's autonomy, since Q has already lost a sufficient degree of social autonomy to P. Hence, Q is no longer a coercee because Q no longer exists as an individual will. On the other hand, if Q retains inde-pendence and social autonomy from P's attempt to control Q or q, Q is again not a victim of coercion. For P (i.e., officials of the Nazi system) to control Q's (i.e., the war criminal's) actions and thence coerce them, P's coercing action(s) must be sufficient to cause Q's doing q (i.e., com-mitting a war crime). That is, Q could not have done otherwise.

In this sense, Q may have done what he or she is charged with doing, but Q cannot be held responsible because P, not Q, controlled his or her own action(s). Q could not have done otherwise because Q lacked sufficient social autonomy to do so. An illustration should elucidate this point.

Nazi judicial decrees were directed against Jewish citizens within Germany and all occupied territories. These decrees included restrictions on housing, mandatory removal from jobs, prohibitions against 'mixed' marriages, mandatory property transfers and confiscations, ghettoization, forced labor, movement restrictions, and deportations.[6]

To support some of these decrees, the Nazis held citizens legally liable to enforce them. For example, under serious penalty, an individual was required to identify his Jewish neighbor to the Nazi authorities.[7] As there is no moral authority *obligating* a person to give up his or her own life for that of another, it would seem understandable prima facie to report one's neighbor, even knowing that neighbor's likely fate. Indeed, if there is evidence in support of the contention that a "supposed offender" was, in a particular instance, deprived of autonomy and thus coerced to commit an offense, it should be sufficient justification to absolve the "supposed offender" from guilt for the offense in question.

However, there are many known instances where non-Jewish persons not only refused to tell the Nazi authorities about their Jewish neighbors but also tried to protect them in the face of 'legal' threats. Whatever may be said about the courage and moral righteousness of these individuals, their behavior attests to the preservation of social autonomy in these cases: Where choices existed, control over one's actions and moral decisionmaking were possible even in the face of attempts at legal and quasi-legal coercion.[8]

Suspected Nazi war criminals and their apologists cannot therefore assume that the argument for coercion is just cause for absolution from a "guilty" verdict or even from undergoing the prosecution process. In virtually all known and documented cases, there is a clear lack of evidence supporting the general claim that the Nazis controlled the actions of these individuals and so caused them to commit war crimes. On the contrary, evidence was brought to bear that these offenders could make choices and for whatever reasons were clearly not prevented from doing otherwise.[9]

Hence examples exist to demonstrate that certain individuals retained sufficient autonomy over their actions, whereas others, perhaps, did not and were in fact coerced. In the former instance, the socially autonomous offender must be held responsible, morally and legally; in the latter case, the coercee may be excused from responsibility. Neither should be excused from the prosecution process. If it can be shown that the suspect did commit the offense, the burden of proof is on the offender to show in a court of law that the offending act was committed under coercion.[10]

THE "CONTRITION" ARGUMENT

There are two sorts of 'contrition' claims mentioned in connection with Nazi war crimes; these claims have some bearing on the current issue about whether to prosecute suspected Nazi war criminals. The first is exemplified by a Nazi soldier who expressed regret at his own criminal behavior and who sought forgiveness from survivors and from others whom he had injured.[11] In assessing a 'contrition' argument against prosecution, it is necessary to distinguish only between genuine contrition and motives for regret that stem from the Reich's failure to succeed. Realistically, the 'contrition' argument in any of its forms stands in bold contrast to the far more common situation: the unrepentant Nazi. Klaus Barbie's attitude toward his conviction for war crimes, particularly murder, typifies that of most Nazis. On receiving a life sentence, Barbie reportedly asserted: "What is there to regret? . . . I am proud to have been a commanding officer of the best military outfit [the Nazi Gestapo] in the Third Reich, and if I had to be born a thousand times again, I would be a thousand times what I have been."[12] His words followed him to his grave (he died in September 1991) and seem to echo the popular sentiments of most Germans and Austrians who prefer to bury their countries' Nazi past and forget it (along with their own roles in persecution or in silence and inaction in the face of evil). Unfortunately, a series of events in Germany in 1992, particularly the violence directed against foreigners living and working there, is being carried out under the banner of making Germany "foreigner free." The widespread sympathy among many segments of the German population for this approach suggests, among other things, that Nazi sentiments may again be flourishing in the new generation of Germans.

A further indication of how rare 'contrition' is likely to be among the ordinary Germans and Austrians who lived in the heartland of Nazism—and who seem to have raised many in the newer generation with a pronounced predisposition to distance themselves from a full and proper account of the Nazi past of their respective countries—is suggested in a number of works in 1991 and 1992. For example, one study exposes the mythical nature of the often-heard claim by Austrians (and others) that they did not know what the Nazis were doing. The fact is that ordinary townspeople living near death camps did know but were appallingly insensitive and apathetic in the face of evil, hence the desire to evade and blot out the past and their complicity in evil.[13] Another study, in 1990, discloses that "many central European rescuers [of Jews] suffered harsh social ostracism for their acts, even after the war"; some suffered milder forms of ridicule, and others' rescue efforts in saving Jews were met with neither comment nor admiration.[14]

In any case, the second 'contrition' claim issues from some who believe that continuing investigations and prosecutions of suspected Nazi war criminals should be halted because these people have already suffered enough for their wrongful acts, i.e., by having to endure the weight of a guilty conscience.[15] Of course, the presumptions behind this claim are that a suspected Nazi war criminal (1) feels guilty, (2) experiences 'guilt' as a form of punishment for wrongdoing, and (3) is being further punished by subjection to a 'prosecution process.'

In our constitutional democracy the 'rule of law' is supremely valued. Those who deliberately violate important laws of society are believed to owe a special debt to the society in the context of the advantages they are assumed to have received. Hence the 'contrition' argument implies that contrition is sufficient payment for an important social debt.[16]

The 'contrition' argument against prosecution is the weakest of the three major arguments because its focus is on the perpetrator's presumed subjective state of mind, instead of on his or her (objective) actions or circumstances of behavior. It seeks neither to deny that the wrongdoing had occurred nor to affirm that the circumstances are personally exculpatory.

The thrust of this argument is an attempt to place the self-professed criminal wrongdoer beyond the reach of the 'prosecution process.' It stresses the disutility of the 'prosecution process' itself by appealing to an unusual view of it, viz., it is a form of unnecessary and additional punishment for offenders who feel guilty for wrongful actions and who regret having done them and who seek forgiveness. In the colloquial sense, many of life's experiences may be 'punishing,' such as inclement weather, a bad grade on an exam, an unwanted spate of debts, and even a judicial process that one may be compelled to undergo. But this colloquial meaning is ultimately different from the notion of punishment as understood in the context of a judicial proceeding, i.e., legal punishment is supposed to be a prescribed official and justly deserved infliction of harm on an offender for legal wrongdoing. The latter evokes the matter of 'just dessert' and harm for a legal infraction whereas the former colloquial sense may refer only to the infliction of pain, whether deserved or not. Hence to collapse this distinction as the contrition argument appears to do is unjustified.

What is generally meant by the term 'contrition'? It refers to a 'sense of guilt' for one's wrongful behavior or to 'guilt feelings' so deep as to alter one's beliefs or lifestyle. Accordingly, a distinction between 'feeling/ being guilty' and 'expressing guilt at the wrongness of one's conduct' seemingly advances the 'contrition' argument because it shows a way to atone or to make restitution and to convince society that restitution is being made without the offender's having to endure the 'prosecution process.' The offender only needs to express a proportionate measure of contrition.

It is tempting to agree that the burden of a guilty conscience, apart from genuine expressions of contrition, is a form of restitution (to society, victims, God, and so on) for having done wrong. This statement may or may not be so, but in any case prosecutors do not seek restitution for Nazi crimes but rather a judicial finding of actual guilt. Governments may, of course, decide to award restitution for political reasons. Only after a legal finding or political admission of wrongdoing does the question of restitution arise along with other possible 'punitive' considerations. If contrition were solely a personal matter of asking forgiveness and being forgiven, no judicial proceeding would be necessary but only a proven technique for measuring genuine contrition, thus engaging a process of atonement.

The appropriate response by society to contrition will depend on the object of contrition and also on who is authorized in particular to evaluate the genuineness of contrition or to respond by acts of forgiveness. If the wrongdoer's 'state of mind' (i.e., guilt feelings, desire for atonement, and so on) is the single most important factor in contrition and forgiveness, any accepted or preferred authority such as parents, teachers, clergy, or God may absolve one's guilt for actually doing wrong. Wrongdoing of a trivial and not illegal kind may justify such recourse, especially if performed from the wrongdoer's mere ignorance, poor judgment, or selfish egoism.

But suppose that the wrongdoing is of a very serious nature, plainly evil or immoral, and illegal, as in the case of Nazi war criminals. Is the 'state of mind' of the wrongdoer the crucial factor in any contrition argument against prosecution? A rebuttal will specify other indispensable considerations involving Nazi war crimes and the 'prosecution process' that must be included in addition to the perpetrator's own current mental state.

There are at least two relevant reasons for being genuinely contrite: (1) Once the offender understands the unacceptable nature of his previous acts, the offender may regret having done them because the acts are no longer tolerable as deviations from the offender's sense of 'good' or 'right'; and (2) a later rejection of the beliefs or ideas that led to the now unacceptable behavior disposes the holder to regret having behaved badly under the old beliefs or ideas.

Furthermore, let us suppose that former Nazi war criminals were genuinely contrite. Is prosecution a justified response, or is 'contrition' entirely irrelevant as to whether suspected Nazi war criminals ought to be prosecuted?

In the unlikely occurrence of a suspected Nazi war criminal's genuine contrition, an appropriate response involves much more than doing what is necessary to relieve the wrongdoer's 'guilt feelings.' Otherwise, if it is mainly a personal or trivial matter, prosecution is clearly excessive since it would be neither necessary nor even effective as a best way to relieve 'guilt feelings' nor would it have reasonable deterrence value; and no law or public policy would be obviously offended by a failure to prosecute. Indeed, nobody but the wrongdoer and a few victims may be aware of or even care about the wrongs done. This response to trivial matters, however, does not apply in the cases of suspected Nazi war criminals, for their crimes were so serious that genuine contrition alone may not be adequately addressed even by a judicial proceeding. In fact, the process of prosecution, conviction, and punishment for more ordinary serious crimes continues to raise questions about whether the genuinely contrite wrongdoer has made adequate restitution for having gone through it. Conviction and punishment for serious wrongdoing are essentially measures to satisfy the victim's and society's need to restore a prior 'moral' balance and 'rule of law' as well as to repay an important social debt.

In showing the weakness of the 'contrition' argument, the intention is not to suggest that if only former Nazi war criminals were genuinely contrite or could be rehabilitated to feel contrite, then the argument against prosecution would hold. In some religious circles, contrition, perhaps combined with some form of penitence to heal the wrongdoer's soul, is sufficient to warrant a pardon from clerical authority. However, a system governed by the 'rule of law' requires an independent judgment rendered in a judicial proceeding to determine legal culpability in cases of serious criminal wrongdoing because it is not only the wrongdoer's soul but also the integrity of the community that needs "salvation." The standard way in which a constitutional democracy such as ours expresses its collective 'legal' entitlement and judgment about serious crimes (which may include at the end an official pardon) is to prosecute the suspected criminal.[17]

To my knowledge there are no known instances where a Nazi war criminal officially accused of serious wrongdoing, formally asked for mercy as a plea against *prosecution* while, of course, admitting guilt. Ordinarily, mercy is a matter for judicial discretion or for consideration by political authorities somewhere down the line in the criminal justice process. It is a plea entered by a convicted defendant who seeks a measure of leniency or kindness (charity) in the determination of punishment (e.g., length of incarceration) beyond what justice requires or the wrongdoer deserves or what can be expected. It is true enough that the demands of justice are rigorous and must be met in a manner that is clearly compatible with its highest ideals. And yet, as the religious tradition of Judaism (and others) teaches, justice must be tempered sometimes with mercy.[18] However, it is far from clear as a general rule when a consideration of mercy merely tempers the severity of justice without also undermining or betraying it. "Temperings are tamperings," one noted philosopher has observed.[19] Accordingly, mercy ultimately may be an injustice.

In the situation I have been addressing justice surely requires the prosecution of such serious offenders as Nazi murderers. Therefore, a connection must be established between "justice" and "mercy" in a sense that does not force us to set aside justice in the interest of mercy, particularly as a moral-religious bar to prosecuting Nazi war criminals. In my view, a decision to leave a Nazi war criminal unprosecuted as a show of mercy is a serious injustice, thereby stigmatizing 'mercy' as having a pejorative, and not ennobling, outcome. I raise this issue in light of the following case.

The distinguished pursuer of Nazi war criminals, Simon Wiesenthal, a man whose eighty-nine-member family was wiped out by the Nazis, has never allowed "mercy" for a prospective Nazi defendant to dissuade him from 'doing justice' by presenting his cases to the appropriate authorities for prosecution. For it has always been his operating principle that he will invariably prosecute if he has the evidence. However, there is one instance where he decided to *not prosecute a Nazi murderer*. Wiesenthal explores this case in his book *Max and Helen*.[20] For my present purpose, it raises the interesting question about the connection between "justice" and "mercy" and whether justice can be taken seriously if tempered by mercy. If justice requires the prosecution of Nazi war criminals who if convicted receive their just desserts as prescribed by law, then any deviation from justice requires a defense because it will prima facie offend justice. Obvious examples of offenses to justice will include "cruel and unusual punishment" of the guilty but also permitting a murderer to go unpunished and thereby depriving society of inflicting on him his just desserts because of the harm done by the offender to society. Therefore, letting a Nazi war criminal go unpunished, even unprosecuted, is a most serious offense against justice and the rule of law.

The case cited by Wiesenthal involves "Max" and "Helen," two pre-war affianced and later survivors of a Ukrainian Nazi concentration camp at Zalesie, and her son (who was born at the war's end). For dramatic details of the case, I refer the reader to Wiesenthal's work. Suffice it to mention that the case is highly idiosyncratic, which is what it must be in order for Wiesenthal not to treat it as he has all the hundreds of others. Indeed, it was not mere idiosyncracy but rather the compelling, life-affirming "mercy" for the lives of the two witnesses ("Max" and "Helen") against the accused, and not for the accused, that tempered his pursuit of justice in not prosecuting this single Nazi murderer. This case has several distinguishing elements: (1) It is an instance where a consideration of mercy is applied to witnesses to murder and not to a prospective defendant or to a person whose guilt has been proven in a court of law;

(2) "mercy" is used to deflect prosecution of an accused Nazi war criminal and not to mitigate punishment after conviction; and (3) it is conceded that the accused will indirectly and inevitably benefit from "mercy" shown to the witnesses against him in that he escapes prosecution (and the possibility of punishment).

In view of these elements, I will make several observations necessary to show the nonarbitrariness of Wiesenthal's decision and how the integrity of the notion of justice I have been discussing is preserved despite his decision to not prosecute. I believe his decision surely results in a serious injustice but not as serious an injustice as would unavoidably occur if consideration of justice were to be reserved only to the accused. It is both persuasively clear and inevitable that an even greater injustice would occur if the prosecution went forward. It would be an injustice to the two witnesses and to the woman's son since it would permanently deprive them of the dignity, self-respect, and enduring love that became absolutely essential to their survival during and especially after the Nazi terror. The circumstances of the case would make this outcome unavoidable.

Wiesenthal is not only talking about the pain and rage (which are unbearable enough) that the judicial process always provokes in all witnesses against their tormentors. He is talking about the assured destruction of what remains of their lives if they testify in open court. This is not a usual nor inexorable consequence for eyewitnesses who testify in these types of proceedings. Reliving the "Night," as Elie Wiesel calls it, is bad enough, but it is not permanently destructive of the very basis of continued survival; in the unusual case of "Max" and "Helen" (and her son), it would be.

Although justice has, in effect, been set aside by mercy, it is not a merciful consideration for the Nazi murderer but for the witnesses against him. The *reason* for setting aside justice with respect to the accused concerns solely a matter of greater injustice to Holocaust victims that would inevitably ensue from prosecution. Therefore, "mercy" shown to prevent an even greater injustice does not really set aside justice but rather ennobles its spirit and as well those who pursue justice for reasons of justice and not mere vengeance. In other words, sensitivity to justice (i.e., taking justice seriously) may require preventing a greater injustice from occurring if respect for the letter is consistently allowed to take precedence over the spirit of justice.[21] It is a reason of justice to use mercy to prevent a greater injustice. In conclusion, I believe that Wiesenthal's *Max and Helen* represents a case of justice and mercy that avoids "unjustified sentimentality, virtuous behavior that is simply a matter of justice, or situations where the demands of justice are thought to be overridden by the demands of utility."[22] Thus there seems to be no sufficient reason to believe that retributive justice and mercy, in my sense, are commensurable values such that conflicts between them are ultimately reconcilable. It may be that they are not reconcilable, as I have suggested, notwithstanding the claims from religious traditions. In any case, I think that Wiesenthal's case illustrates the unresolvability of this conflict unless mercy—as in this case—is bestowed for an even more important reason of justice, viz., preventing a greater injustice.[23] Finally, this case shows just how extraordinary it must be in order to avoid prosecution in the interest of compassion for the victims; for by not doing a greater injustice, the priority of justice in prosecuting Nazi war criminals is sustained and, indeed, strengthened, since no other instance of serious offenders is known to have sufficiently similar circumstances. That is, it is the exception proving the rule.

SUMMARY

The arguments discussed here have been labeled (1) the "passage of time" argument, (2) the "extenuating circumstances" argument, and (3) the "contrition" argument. Each, with its particular variations, describes the sorts of undesirable and weighty consequences that its proponents believe would flow from ignoring the argument's ultimate point and pleas, viz., to not prosecute suspected Nazi war criminals. It has been my task in the foregoing analysis of these positions and their respective ramifications to marshall the sort of arguments that best rebut these positions. Although some arguments are simply invalid, certain others may be successfully used to temper punishments or even to absolve suspects from guilt or responsibility in cases where convincing evidence can be shown. However, none of the arguments can be shown to be sufficient cause to stop the 'process of prosecution.'

Thus I do not contend that all who are prosecuted must be found guilty or even that all who deserve punishment for moral/legal offenses must receive equal penalties or even penalties proportionate to the crime or *necessarily* some punishment, though such is arguably warranted. Rather it is my minimalist thesis that suspected Nazi war criminals ought to suffer some public trial in which to answer for their alleged criminal wrongdoing wherein the various excuses and explanations offered by them and by their supporters can be sorted out and thoroughly examined on a case-by-case basis.

Since Nazi persecution, especially organized and deliberate mass murder, is never a private but a public matter for civilized society, the obligation to consider punishment for convicted wrongdoers or at least to prosecute the suspected criminals is for official or public authorities to sponsor. Governments and their judicial agencies and international tribunals duly constituted to carry through such proceedings are the public bodies on whom this obligation falls. It is as morally wrong for them not to enact laws enabling them to prosecute similar wrongdoers in the future as not to prosecute those who have evaded justice for so long, and it is wrong for citizens not to persuade their governments to do so. For this is consistent with a most important meaning of civilization as a moral community, or at least as the way to take moral and legal obligations seriously.

NOTES

1. The election of Kurt Waldheim to the Austrian presidency on June 8, 1986, and the groundswell of popular support for him, in full view of the disclosures about his Nazi past, is to be noted. In addition, the widespread support Chancellor Helmut Kohl received in Germany about President Ronald Reagan's visit to the Bitburg Cemetery where SS are buried is perhaps indicative of how 'guilty' the new generation feels and raises a set of questions about the lack of breadth of knowledge and the lack of sensitivity of German youth to the Holocaust. In the United States, a notorious group has formed in California calling itself the Institute for Historical Review. Its main preoccupation: the "mythical Jewish Holocaust." Its leading publication: *Debunking the Genocide Myth: The Hoax of the 20th Century*. This group seeks complete exculpation of the alleged offenders by a denial that the Holocaust ever occurred. For the argument that too little time has passed to scrutinize fairly the Nazi atrocities (but too much time to prosecute wrongdoers), see Gordon J. Horwitz, *In the Shadow of Death: Living Outside the Gates of Mauthausen* (New York: Free Press, 1990), pp. 183–86.

2. Peter Schneider, *The German Comedy* (New York: Farrar, Straus and Giroux, 1991), pp. 189–90.

3. Criminal prosecution for any offense in the United States punishable by death, particularly murder, may be initiated against the suspected wrongdoer at any time sans limitation, except for offenses barred. See the federal statute 18 U.S.C.A. Sec. 3281; nor is there a statute of limitations for prosecution concerning lying on one's citizenship application. Despite its checkered history, statutes of limitations regarding war crimes and crimes against humanity have been abolished in a number of countries including Germany (formerly the Federal Republic of Germany). Romania, however, abolished its laws for prosecuting and punishing Nazi war criminals (in 1955). See *Encyclopedia of the Holocaust*, vol. 4 (New York: Macmillan, 1990), pp. 1507 and 1518, respectively.

4. Yale Kamisar, Wayne R. LaFave, and Jerold H. Israel, *Basic Criminal Procedure*, 6th ed. (St. Paul: West, 1986), pp. 12–13.

5. See Alan S. Rosenbaum, *Coercion and Autonomy: Philosophical Foundations, Issues, and Practices* (Westport: Greenwood Press, 1986), p. 135.

6. See, e.g., Raul Hilberg, *The Destruction of the European Jews* (New York: Harper Torchbooks, 1961), pp. 116, 118.

7. See Glenn Collins, "Women in Nazi Germany: Paradoxes," *New York Times*, March 1, 1987, p. 15.

8. See John Martin Fischer, "Responsibility and Control," in J. M. Fischer, ed., *Moral Responsibility* (Ithaca: Cornell University Press, 1986), p. 181. Published testimony by a number of SS officers makes it clear that a refusal to obey orders involving murder did not usually lead to adverse consequences; see Ernst Klee, Willi Dressen, and Volker Riess, eds., *The Good Old Days* (New York: Free Press, 1991), pp. 75-86.

9. Eugene Davidson, *The Trial of the Germans* (New York: Collier Books, 1966), pp. 3–9, 39–58, 583. Also, see Robert J. Lifton, *The Nazi Doctors* (New York: Basic Books, 1986), pp. 452–58, 464–65, 488–93. A discussion of the psychology and training of physicians who readily internalized the "psychology of genocide" and performed "medical killing" is included.

10. For reactions and defenses by the Nuremberg defendants, see Robert E. Conot, *Justice at Nuremberg* (New York: Harper and Row, 1983), pp. 56–58, 105, 492–523.

11. Simon Wiesenthal, *The Sunflower* (New York: Shocken Books, 1976).

12. *Plain Dealer* (Cleveland), September 26, 1991; also, *New York Times*, September 26, 1991, p. C19.

13. See Gordon J. Horwitz, *In the Shadow of Death*, pp. 181–83.

14. Kristen R. Monroe, Michael C. Barton, and Ute Klingemann, "Altruism and the Theory of Rational Action: Rescuers of Jews in Nazi Europe," *Ethics*, vol. 101, no. 1 (October, 1990), p. 109.

15. Allan A. Ryan, Jr., *Quiet Neighbors* (New York: Harcourt Brace Jovanovich, 1984), pp. 244–45, 336.

16. A variation of this claim is discussed in connection with capital punishment, but here also it fails to answer a question about the purpose of the 'rule of law'; see Susan Jacoby, *Wild Justice* (New York: Harper and Row, 1983), p. 6.

17. For an account of historical war crimes that also undercuts the "contrition" argument, see Emil L. Fackenheim "Responses to the Holocaust," *Holocaust and Genocide Studies*, vol. 1, no. 1 (1986), pp. 110–12.

18. W. Gunther Plautz, Bernard J. Bamberger, and William W. Hallow, *The Torah: A Modern Commentary* (New York: Union of American Hebrew Congregations, 1981), pp. 1461–62.

19. Jeffrie G. Murphy, "Mercy and Legal Justice," in Jeffrie G. Murphy and Jean Hampton, *Forgiveness and Mercy* (New York: Cambridge University Press, 1988), p. 167.

20. Simon Wiesenthal, *Max and Helen* (New York: Morrow, 1982).

21. 'Injustice' in this normative sense is a type of serious harm or deep wrong done to someone. For instance, see Joel Feinberg's discussion of harm in *Harm to Others*, vol. 1 (New York: Oxford University Press, 1987), p. 34.

22. Murphy and Hampton, *Forgiveness and Mercy*, p. 173.

23. See the discussion in R. A. Duff, "Justice, Mercy, and Forgiveness," *Criminal Justice Ethics*, vol. 9, no. 2 (Summer-Fall, 1990), pp. 62–63.

ABOUT THE BOOK AND AUTHOR

It has been nearly fifty years since the collapse of the Nazi regime; is there any longer a point to presenting for the apprehension and prosecution of surviving Nazi war criminals?

In this carefully argued book, Alan Rosenbaum makes it clear that there is. He contends that apart from concerns about obligations to the dead or vengeance against the living, we must continue to pursue the prosecutorial agenda as an investment in the moral climate in which we wish to live. To fail to do so would be to fail in our commitment to a society safe for ethnic, cultural, and religious diversity.

Demonstrating that the crucial arguments apply well beyond the specific concern about war criminals, Rosenbaum looks at other current issues, including the treatment of hate groups and hate speech, the ideas and cultural contributions of antisemites, and the reconstruction of a Christian theology without antisemitism.

This book is an important contribution to Jewish and Holocaust studies, to political and social thought, and to moral theory.

Alan S. Rosenbaum is associate professor at Cleveland State University and the author of several books and articles on human rights and political theory.

INDEX